THROUGH THE EYES OF A CHILD

Gloria Wynter Christ

with Dr. Curt Wagner

And Ronald Ellyson

Dedication

This book is dedicated to the Jewish couple who fed me as a child; to my daughter, Monique Campbell; to my departed son, Darlus Campbell; to my youngest son, Lesroy Wynter, and his wife, Chaniqua Wynter; to my four grandchildren; to my nephew Kincade Douglas; Also My 'adopted parents' (through ("**Father. Yah'uah**") Dr. Curt and Gretchen Wagner, and to their son, Ben; also to Roger and Sheila Rice. There are a whole lot of people I would like to give thanks and praise to, but I cannot because I may leave someone out and feelings would be hurt. And I would like to thank the city of Hinesville for helping me grow as a person, and 'Dragon Naturally Speaking' for making a software product that has allow me to have a voice so that I could tell my whole story which is a collection of memories (at least most of what I can remember). Also Dr. Seth A. Borquaye, Misty Young, and Dr. Richard Anderson who for years walked me through those dark alleyways of my mind to find the truth that I kept trying to hide from 'God.' Father Yah'uah He knew I was in there and he and a whole lot of others who helped me find myself

Preface

This is my third time writing this manuscript. It has been lost twice in the computer and thrown away. Several times I have had the urge to drink while writing it, or to go dancing, and sometimes I just sit and cry. I have isolated myself from friends and family. This book is not to make you sad nor to horrify you and certainly not to take your faith away, but to show that no matter what, **"Father Yah'uah"** *Elohim* ('God') is there always helping you. It is for the people who are in my life today and for the people who have moved on. It is for the people who poured well into my life and the people who poured evil into my life. It is for family and friends that I am with and without. It is for the ones who have gone home to be with **"Father Yah'uah"** *Elohim* and *"Yah'shua"* His only-begotten Son the Messiah ('Jesus' the 'Christ'). That is to say they have all played a special part in my life by helping me grow. Those of you who have opened a whole new world for me by giving me a chance to grow into the real person I was meant to be, you have helped shape me into the woman I am today. Those of you who have pointed me in the direction of **"Father Yah'uah"** *Elohim* and *"Yah'shua"* he Messiah—whether you were good or bad, whether short-term or long-term— you were there to bring change into my life and to help guide me into the plans of **"Father Yah'uah"** and in the seventh of the Messiah without all of you I do not know if I would have known my Messiah *"Yah'shua"* the Son, are we're I would have ended up. I constantly give "**Father Yah'uah**" the glory. To me He is more than I could have ever imagined a 'Father' could be. I truly believe by now I would've been dead if it had not been for Father Yah'uah working through some of the most amazing people he put in my life so he could save me. I am so sorry my brothers and sisters did not get a chance to know "Father **Yah'uah**" and "*Yah'shua the Messiah*" as I do and how much love Father Yah'uah and Yah;shua the Messiah has for them.

Prologue

Mama picked me up. She threw me down the cellar steps. I was unconscious. She threw water on me until I woke up. She made all of my brothers and sisters and I dig a hole in the basement. She made me get in a box. I was fighting my brothers and sisters so they could not put me in the box. My brother 'Sonny' was lying on top of me and said, "'Peewee', stop fighting us. I will come and get you out of the box." Then Mama nailed the box shut. She made my brothers and sisters put the box in the hole in a whole and the basement floor. They had to cover it up with dirt from the basement floor. Then she left the house for a long time. As soon as she left, 'Sonny,' Barbara Jean, 'Hot Mama,' and Deborah dug me out of that hole. Was the 'Holy Spirit' of *Elohim Father Yah'uah* guiding them? Now that I am older and I think about it! Yes he was, how else could four small children using only their bare hands dig me out of the hole in the basement that took all 20 children to dig? It had to be the 'Holy Spirit' of Father Yah'uah somehow guiding my 4 brothers and sisters to save me.

My Family

I do not know where to really begin, so I will begin right here and right now. I was born Gloria Mae Stewart to Barbara Stewart. I had 17 brothers and sisters: Carl, Ray, Edley and Teddy, Dale and Cynthia, Barbara Jean and Steve (who was called 'Sonny'), my twin sister who died (I am not really sure if she was really my twin sister because it did not say so on the birth certificate 'two baby girls'), Gale Christine (who was called 'Hot Mama'), Deborah, (we called her 'Debe'), Adriana (who was called 'Koochie Mama'), David and his twin brother (I do not know David's twin brother's name; he died) and a set of twin boys who died (I do not know their names), and my baby brother Harold.

Barbara Stewart was not my mama's real name but it would be 38 years before I learned what her real name was. I found out what my mama really name was because I wanted to know who I really was and who she really was, so I began looking for my mama's family. My mama got sick and had to go to Savannah where she had a sister named Edna. My mama's sister told me my mama's real name. My Aunt Edna said, "Your mama's real name is Dorothy Jean Bohannon." She asked my mama, "How come your child don't know their mama's real name or your birth place or how old you are Jean? For sure" We did not know it; not one of us knew who she really was. In 2008 I learned my mama's age. My mama was born on March 2, 1931. Our mama had lots of names that she used when she stole money from the government, meaning the welfare department, and she used different men's' names on our birth certificates. These men who were not our fathers, they were just made-up names of men. During that time all the women did that sort of thing to keep the real fathers from paying any type of child support and to boost their welfare checks. I really did not have my own birth certificate until I was 33 years old. Well, it really wasn't a birth certificate. It was a piece of paper to say I was born a United States citizen and who I am. It gave my name and the city I was born in, not very much information beyond that. It was just something else to take my real identity from me; it is as though I really did not exist. And most of the time that is how I feel.

Consequences of Abuse

We were invisible children without a voice and stripped of all human feelings; we were unknown, uncared-for and unloved. It may seem to you the reader that this story is fiction, but I assure you it is not and I'm telling you the truth. It's a true story. It happened to me and my brothers and sisters. But first I need to explain what happens to you when you are abused like we were. When a rapist rapes you, he or she says to you, "You cannot tell anybody about it at all." So it buries who you are and kills who you are supposed to be. Something begins to grow inside of you; it is growing at an unbelievable speed; it's there ripping you apart. It is an ugly sauce of scarring and lying, always hurting, hating, distrusting, you become so full of anger, and violence, self-pity and hatred of your own self and others. The original innocence is replaced by a hideous 'monster' which refuses to leave and which seeks someone or something to prey on, so that the person becomes capable of murder of others or even oneself. They cannot feel your pain, or their own as time goes by. They become hopeless and loveless wanderers of the dark, always plotting, always fighting, always destroying, and never seeking peace just a festering pot of hate and distrust that grow to loves conflict and war and always ready to fight; and somehow this evil spirit is devouring the innocent child and nothing seems to be able to stop it. What was encased in Mama's soul? Now the evil one who destroyed her soul is destroying the children she brought into the world or had she simply given her soul to the evil one? I wonder some time what had happened to Dorothy Jean Bohannon, what had happened to her to make her become such an enemy to her children, why had life destroyed her? And now she was destroying all of us, all of the children who came out of her own body. She did not do it with her bare hands, but she was the sold instrument that doomed us all. She was the tool of the enemy against us. She made all the decisions on ways to destroy us. Yes it was Mama, no one else, just Mama who held our faith in her hands. She had destroyed us one by one. She had filled us with madness, violence, and hatred. Most children who go through sexual child abuse cannot trust anyone. People like us rather they are a man are a woman when they get married they often cannot completely trust each other, especially around their own children. Self-destruction may come to the marriage even though each of them is 'innocent of doing any wrong to the children.' They cannot trust each other, they are afraid that what their parents had done to them is what they will do to their own children. They may think that their spouse is waiting for the chance to get their child alone so they can do what was done to them. So neither one of them ever learns to trust the one they have fallen in love with. At times they can't stand to even touch their own children because they feel that they are going to do the same thing to their children what had been done to them. Rape does not just happen to women and girls, it also happens to boys and men in it affect them in horrible ways. It happened to my brothers and sisters as well as to me. The tree has caused all of its branches to shrink and fade away, leaving the child mentally and physically very dysfunctional. These children are detached from the rest of the world; they have great big holes in their souls. Not knowing or understanding love, they can't understand how to give love to someone else or how to separate love from lust. Although sexual intimacy was to be shared only between husband and wife, it cannot happen for them because within their hearts hate is sitting in their hearts taking love's place, and it is refusing to depart. So they cannot love at all, and when they're trying very hard to open up to others, they find themselves closing every door so no one will see the monsters which dwell deep down in the depths of their souls. Deep down inside they are crying and shouting, "Someone let me out, I cannot breathe! Please, someone set me free! Someone see me and teach me how to give and receive love, because I don't know what love is"! Oh, how they long to know what real love is, how they long and dream of being free of all the hatred and misery. Day after day, night after night, their souls plead to be set free. "Dear "**Father Yah'uah**" *Elohim*, come to me and set me free; teach me your love so something good can grow inside of me. I desire to know the love of a mother and a father. "Father **Yah'uah**"— you have been all those things to me; your love is calling me. Father, Father Yah'uah — Hurry up, Father Yah'uah, come and save me—can't you see that there is a real person inside of me"?

Love is given freely to all those who desire it. It has nothing to do with sexual intercourse. It is something that only "Father **Yah'uah**" gives so freely! It is for all those who desire it. This gift of love is to be set free from all kinds of misery it is to be shared with all those who would only believe that Yahshua the Messiah died on the cross to set us free. The love between husband and wife is a gift from Father Yah'uah so that the two will become 'one' and so that they will bring forth new life. And that new life is a gift from "Father Yah'uah" that sets the captive free that new life begins to spread like a beautiful tree with all of its branches reaching out for more life. It invites you to ask the Messiah Yah'shua into your life, to ask *"Yah'shua"* the Messiah to be your deliverer and give you knew hope in life.

He will impart this gift to you so the Kingdom of Father Yah'uah *Elohim* is built and sewn together with the fabric of His love for us.

My Mama

I am going to give you a description of what my Mama looked like. She was beautiful, I mean really beautiful! She was a very light-skinned woman. (During that time if you were light-skinned you got most of the men.) She had her hair dyed red and wore it in a long ponytail or pulled up from her face. And she had such a beautiful smile. It was so intriguing. I would sometimes watch Mama for hours, wondering how someone so beautiful could act so ugly. She would not hold me or touch me without hurting me. When she called me or one of my brothers and sisters, we would always crouch down and cover our faces because we did not know what to expect from someone so beautiful. It was sheer terror to come near Mama; you never knew what was about to happen to you. And that was the most terrifying part of all, not knowing what she planned on doing to you next. Mama was uncaring, unloving, unfeeling; she had such a sinister smile, yet she was beautiful. Her beauty was so eerie. My mama could read and write but her children could not because she made us as dumb as rocks when it came to books. She purposely refused to let us learn to read. If we were caught reading a book we were beaten. We were not supposed to know what was in books. Mama made us that way so we could not function without her controlling us. I say that because my oldest sister Barbara Jean had to be told everything she needed to do by Mama or someone else. She could not function on her own, no matter who was in her life; Mama had full control over my sister's life. Ultimately she would play a big part in my sister's losing her life.

My Aunt Edna

I got to know my mama's sister, who lived in Savannah, when I was 38 years old. Although I'd met her I had not talked to her a lot. My mama got sick once; and went to stay with my Aunt Edna who lived in Savannah Georgia. I had not known her well before that but after Mama got sick I began to know and respect my Aunt Edna. She is a wonderful person; I can really say I love her. She was so different than my mama; she treated me with so much love. She'd call me, all the time she'd send me birthday cards, but even today I still get nervous when I talk to her. She brought her sons and daughter to meet me. She has given me some family members' names and telephone numbers. But I have not called any of them except for my cousin who is my Aunt Edna's son, because I do not know them, and I don't know what to say to them. But I really would like to meet all of them so they could give me a sense of where and who I come from—I mean the line of people who are in my bloodline. I think everybody wants to know where they come from, so my heart cries out for that. But time will tell. It has to be "Father **Yah'uah**" *Elohim* who opens up those doors for me. I really love my Aunt Edna. Sometimes I wonder what it would have been like if she had been my mother. She and my Aunt Rosa, both women, are very good women.

Aunt Rosa

My Aunt Rosa used to come to Mama's house to visit us with her husband and her own children, my Uncle Reuben was a Spanish man, and we loved him. My Aunt Rosa was a heavyset lady. She did not know what was going on in Mama's house. When she would come, she would bring all kinds of fruits and vegetables from a farm that she and her husband worked on in New Jersey. She had children of her own, but she was still real good to us. She would feed us breakfast in the morning and give us lunch and give us decent food at night. I can still hear her saying to Mama, "Give those kids some damn water. You get thirsty, don't you, Jean? Who are you saving the damn food for, Jean? These kids are always hungry. And they are as skinny as hell. Don't you feed them?" When it was time to go to bed, she would take all kinds of snacks upstairs and feed them to us while we would snuggle up to her. I would climb on top of her chest; 'Hot Mama,' 'Koochie Mama,' Deborah, 'Sonny,' and Barbara Jean and David and Harold we would be lying on her stomach and legs, plus her own children. She would be saying, "This damn bed is not big enough for all of us!" But she would not put one of us out of the bed. My Uncle Reuben would sleep on the floor next to the bed. When he came in from partying with Mr. Tex my Mama's boyfriend, my Aunt Rosa would say, "I hope you had a good time, Reuben." He would reply, "Yes, yes, Rosa, go to sleep now." If he was out of the house my Aunt Rosa could not sleep until he came back in the house, even if it was daybreak. Most of all she would not let Mama beat us or hit us at all as long as she was there. She would say, "Leave them damn kids alone, Jean. Let them play. You cannot work them all the time." She would make sure we played. She called us 'eating machines.' If she only knew that the only time we ate well was when she was there. The animals were treated like human beings and we were treated worse than animals. And eventually we became aggressive *in as vicious as while animals.*

My Father

I am going to give you a description of my dad. I do not understand why he did not take us away from Mama, or keep my brother 'Sonny' with him. 'Sonny' constantly ran away and went to my father's house. Each time he did my father would bring him back to Mama's house. He would ran away from home and Once he ran away and went to Florida to my grandmother's house, but as always, he was brought back to Mama. This is not what our father should have done; he should have protected us. I kept hoping that my father would take us to live with him so Mama couldn't hurt me and my brothers and sisters. But my dad never did. He knew we loved him; I just don't know why he didn't want us like my sisters Dale and Cynthia father loved them and wanted them to be safe with him. Their fathers came and got them. We never saw them again. They never came and visited us after that. I often think about what really happened to them or if they ever think about us. The men who took them with him, was there father he was a white man, and he kind of looked like them. I can remember thinking one day our father will take us with him but that day never happened. I can remember Mama saying; "Two more gone, eight more to go" and then she would laugh hysterically. Mama would not have just let them go to live with their fathers. He probably had to pay Mama for them, because we were her money-makers. She would say, "Y'all are my money-makers". Sometimes she would say in front of her friends,

"Who are you 'all?" and we would reply, "Your money-makers, Mama."

Our father came once a year. I will give you a description of what my dad looked like. He was about 5 foot 11. He was a light-skinned man and a very handsome man. My father looked like Santa Claus. He had rosy cheeks and very thick eyebrows. His hair was waved naturally, not permed. It had little waves and curls, and he had pretty white teeth. I loved my dad. We would see him once a year and whenever he would come by, he would buy us all kinds of things—clothing, toys, food, and candy—and we tried to eat everything we could before he brought us back to the house to Mama. He would take us to the movies. The first real movie I ever saw was "The Ten Commandments," the first time I ever went to the movies it was with my father. When he left us to go home, Mama would never let us wear or play or eat anything he brought for us. We could not wear the clothing unless we were going to one of her clients' houses. That was the only time we could use the clothing. If we had candy left, Mama would take it and put it out for her clients. We could not even wear the shoes my father brought for us. He never hit us. When he would come to see us, he would bring our two older brothers. I believe their names were Edley and Teddy. I do not know their last names. My father's name was Benson Powell. I believe my brother 'Sonny' told my dad about the beatings and what was happening to us, but he did not take us with him. 'Sonny' had cuts and burn marks all over his body. I know he showed them to my father; I will never understand why my father allowed Mama to beat us the way she did. He didn't see the beatings but he saw us with sores all over our bodies, on our heads, on the bottoms of my feet; he saw these things but said or did nothing to save us from Mama.

The Abuses

This is my very first memory. Mama would put diapers and rubber pants on us to keep us from wetting the baby crib. I heard some sounds that sounded like my mama was crying or being hurt. I thought she was crying so I began to cry as most children would do when they think something is wrong with their mom. The light came on. My Brother David's father—his name was Jimmy James—took me from the baby crib and put me in the bed with him and Mama. He removed my rubber pants and diaper. He proceeded to push his fingers into my body. The sexual acts would escalate. If I began to scream and holler Mama would begin slapping me and choking me. At that time I had to be three or four years old. This would go on until Mama found another man in her life, and the new man would take the place of the old one in bed with one of us. This is my very first memory.

Sometimes these scenes play over and over in my mind like I am seeing things through the eyes of a child, or I can hear myself screaming but not making a sound. I am dying but not dead, clawing the bed trying to breathe in air, because the person on top of me was squeezing out my air. He and Mama would be smothering me with their bodies. The more I squirmed and hollered, the less they cared. One day the hollering just stopped. I could not hear myself making a sound anymore. I was just silent. I could not feel anything, because I was seeing things through the eyes of a child. I was dancing in my head; I was a Princess. I thought it would be easy to tell this story but I am finding out that it is tearing out my heart. But I know also, it is something I have to do. I am finally able to tell what happened to me and my brothers and sisters; I do not have to carry the burden of keeping this secret anymore.

Mama's Parties

My mama had such lavish parties. Mama was the only person at that time that had a big television box. It had a sheet of plastic that went over it. The plastic had four colors on it; the colors were blue, red yellow and green. I am not sure if it was in that order but I know that it was those colors. At the party the people would talk about the television box. They would say, "Barbara you are doing okay. You are doing well. You give the best parties, Barbara." The parties would last all night, until daybreak. There were people everywhere. They were eating steak, chicken, fish, pork chops, spareribs, ham, and mashed potatoes; green peas, corn on the cob, black-eyed peas and rice, okra, collard greens, tomatoes, stuffed eggs, and fudge, you name it. They had all kinds of food and drinks including milk.

But we were kept in a fenced cage with no clothes on. Men and women, black and white, would come and choose what child they were going to sleep with, and Mama made sure she collected all of her money up front. Before the night began, she would tell us exactly how much money to ask them for ourselves; she said, "Tell them you want a tip". But the money was never for us. At the end of the night she would collect all of the money she told us to ask them for. While the people were waiting to have their turn with one of us, they were eating and drinking all kinds of strong drinks. When they were finished eating, they would take their plates and rake and scrape the bones and scrap on the floor inside the fence cage. We would scramble like dogs, fighting one another to eat the bits of crumbs and to suck and chew on bones. When Mama would give us food it was only beans or plain rice. All of this happened under the watchful eyes of our Mama. She kept her beautiful smile on her proud-looking face.

Mama was happy to be alive, her dyed red hair in place and all of her clothing in place on her thin-frame shaped body. Not a wrinkle showed anyplace. Mama was beautiful, and she knew how beautiful she was.

Mama was the only woman in the house who had a watch except for the white women and white men that had watches. Some black men had watches but none of the black women had watches, only Mama. She had all kinds of watches. I liked the gold watches the best. Mama looked so beautiful when gold was against her skin, or she had on her gold bracelets and her gold earrings. No woman in that house could compare to Mama and everybody wanted to be her. She always bragged about how the other ladies wished they were her. She made fun of how they walked and talked and the clothing they wore. Mama said their clothing was cheap and came from the 'five-and-dime' store. Mama said she would "not be caught dead in none of that cheap stuff." She loved to go to the department stores to buy her things, unless one of her customers would trade something to have sex with one of us, especially when the truck drivers or the longshoremen came in to the city. When they came into the city Mama could not wait to show off to her clients and friends the new things they brought for her; that always made Mama real happy. Mama would say, "What you got for me now"? Sometimes it would be whiskey or clothing, sometimes pretty things for the bed like blankets and quilts. Mama always had pretty things.

Mama had lots of jewelry, all kinds of jewelry. She wore large earrings and rings on both hands. Mama even had ankle bracelets. She had lots of gold and silver necklaces Mama even had pearls. I loved to see gold on Mama. Even today I love gold. It looked so beautiful against my mama's beautiful skin. She looked like a movie star, like the people inside of the television box. I thought the people in the television box were real, and Mama had put them inside the television box, and she was the only one who could come out of the television box. I find gold so beautiful and always think about Mama and how it would look against her beautiful skin. She had so much jewelry and yet she had children in the house starving, looking like children from the third-world countries.

Our Living Conditions

Nobody cared for us; nobody changed anything for us. We were so starved that our innards came out of our anuses. We did not chew food. We swallowed food whole. That behavior would go on until I became an adult. 'Christian' people taught me how to chew food; it was Scott and Beverly Phillips who taught me how to chew my food. "**Father Yah'uah**" *Elohim* was working through Scott and Beverly; He was teaching me through them how to chew my food. I just couldn't see Him; working through them. I did not know He was working through Scott and Beverly. Sometimes they had to take my plate from me so I would slow down and chew my food properly. Scott Phillips was in the Army; he would say, "You have to take baby steps; now take a bite and chew it 100 times." I got better at it after awhile, but I still have the tendency to swallow food whole if I get real hungry or become busy and forget to eat. When things like that happen I just swallow. In time I will get better at chewing food. It is typical for children and adults who have been starved to just swallow food whole; they seem to just swallow it down whole; they do not waste time on chewing anything. They just want to feel full. I know all I wanted was to be safe and full; it would be years before I would feel safe. Even today I don't always know when I'm full.

As a child I thought all adults slept with children. We were kept isolated with two buckets in the middle of the floor, one for drinking water and one to use as a toilet. We were mostly kept in the dark. Mama would only turn the lights on to show us to her clients so they could decide which child they were going to sleep with. We had a big bucket of water in the middle of the room. If we knocked over the water, that was it for us. We did not know when we would get more water or food to eat. We really looked like those children you see on television with those big protruding stomachs. Our heads were full of sores. We had cuts and bruises everywhere, cigarette burns all over us. Mama had lots of animals. She had cats and dogs, goldfish, pop-eyed fish, kissing fish, angelfish, sunfish, and many others. She had rabbits, a snake, frogs, and turtles; she even had house mice as pets. We had to make sure they were kept clean and fed, and water was in their bowls. We had to clean up any 'mistakes' the animals might have made in the house.

Mama's animals had their own food but her children only had scraps and bones, or beans and sometimes rice when she would remember to feed us. We would eat the dog food and the cat food, steal the dogs' bones and drink the cats' milk if there was no water in the bucket upstairs. We would come downstairs and drink the cats' or dogs' water. We were not allowed to go into the kitchen cabinet and Mama kept a long chain around the refrigerator. We were not allowed to go downstairs and get a glass of water. We were too afraid to turn on the water, because we knew if Mama came home and found the kitchen sink wet she would beat us; she had done that so many times before. So we would just drink the dogs' and cats' water or milk.

The 'Jewish' Couple

When Mama would leave we would go into our backyard and eat the grapes off of our neighbor's grapevine and suck the juice from the flowers of the honeysuckle tree I would climb over the fence into the neighbor's backyard, then go into their garbage cans and eat any food in the garbage cans. If one of us did not climb that fence, he or she did not eat. An older married 'Jewish' couple was living about three houses down from our house the wife would put a pan of food on the ground for me by her door. She did not let me into her home, but every time I climbed that fence she had that pan of food there for me. One day I climbed over the fence and she was not at the door for me. Her husband was rushing her to fix the food for me but she was moving too slow for him. He grabbed the pan and fixed the food for me and put it on the ground. He never looked directly at me; he raised his arm and covered his face, stooped down, and placed the pan on the ground. You could hear him weeping as he waved his hand, not for me to go but for me to eat. I have a deep love for the 'Jewish' people; **"Father Yah'uah"** was there in that husband and wife for the last eleven years. I give $100 each month, (and anything extra I get) to help bring 'Jewish' people back to Israel and to help feed the elderly there. I always remember how that elderly couple fed me. It was the husband and wife who saved my life by filling my belly; this is one way I know how to pay back the 'Jewish' people for what that couple did for me. Was Father Yah'uah there in their lives yes he was working to them to save me.

Our Diet

This is how Mama gave us food. It was for her and her clients' amusement; they would bet on which one of us would be able to beat the other child in a fight so we could have that plate of food. We were taught how to fight each other. Mama would place a plate of beans or rice at the doorway of the fenced cage and put two of us in the cage. We would bite, scratch, pull out each other's hair and stomp one another. We would box each other silly for that plate of rice or beans. As an adult I would never give my children beans. If they had them, someone else gave them beans. But I would not. And only once have I ever allowed my children to fight each other.

Sexual Abuse

My brother 'Sonny' had to sleep with men and women. He also had to sleep with us for my Mama's amusement or if one of her clients requested it. 'Sonny' was 11 months older than I. He did not have a choice of what went on in Mama's house. By the time I was four years old 16 of us had to go to the Department of Health in New York City on J Street, because all the children in our house had sexually transmitted diseases. Actually there were 20 children living in the house. I know because we had to do a countdown, and it would always stop at 20. The other children were named Mary, Gwendolyn and Ronnie; there was another child who was blind and deaf whose name I don't remember. There were children always coming and going; people would take them and never bring them back. Sometimes when they came back Mama would say, "You are not good for nothing now" and we would not see them anymore. I do not know what happened to them Lots of times the person who took them would come back for a different child or I would hear them and Mama fussing over the price she wanted for that particular child.

The first time I saw someone having oral sex with a child was Mama; she made us stand and watch her make my oldest sister Barbara Jean have oral sex with her. I will never forget the look on Barbara Jean's face when it was over; it was a look of total defeat. She had nothing to live for and nothing to fight for. I can still see her face today, the way her face looked. All of us would have to do the same thing; Mama would make us have sex with her and whoever was her boyfriend at that time.

Children are a gift from "**Father Yah'uah**" *Elohim*, but my mama yielded us to Satan. She made choices for us. It has helped me to understand why Sodom and Gomorrah were destroyed along with all the children in it. It is all about what you yield your bodies to. Read the whole story about Lot and his family [Genesis 19]. Lot got out of Sodom and Gomorrah, but his two daughters got him drunk and had sexual intercourse with him. They had picked up the ways of the people they were living near. I was always afraid I was going to be just like Mama, because people would say I looked a little bit like her. I just was not pretty like my Mama was.

I believe "**Father Yah'uah**" is waiting to change our lives. There were all kinds of signs He was there; I just didn't know He was there waiting for me to seek Him and decide to know Him. Some people commit acts of sexual perversion but do not become self-destructive, because they know they are already walking dead; they are breathing air but they are dead to the world. They become heartless towards others. They have self-pity. They cannot see "**Father Yah'uah**" *Elohim* acting to set them free. They become accusers of "Father Yah'uah and Yah'shua the Messiah rather than Satan there life becomes devoted to serving the evil one. And if they are children their lives have ended before it began. They are with the same spirits that lived long ago in Sodom and Gomorrah; lust is their passion and Satan is their 'God.' The word of "**Father Yah'uah**" *Elohim* says, "Train up a child in the way he should go" [Prov. 22:6]. So if you bring up a child in the ways of Satan, isn't that the way most of them will go? These people are tearing down themselves and others most of the time, instead of building them up. All it would take is a drop of hate to tear down anything that was built up. I know because I lived it.

Our Thievery

In my Mama's house we had all kinds of lessons. She taught us how to shimmy down a roof, break into the neighbor's house, and open a window with a spoon; how to steal food from grocery stores and to take only the meats you were instructed to. The meats were steaks, roast beef, fresh ham, smoked ham, chicken, ground beef, fish and pork chops. If you came home with luncheon meat, chicken backs, chicken necks, pigs' feet or pigs' ears, you were in for the beating of your life. Mama wouldn't cook those types of food for her clients but on holidays she cooked those meats for us. Then she would get mad at us and throw everything in the garbage can. We would just wait until her clients started coming in and then we would go downstairs to the garbage can and eat the food. When she sent you to steal, there were certain things she wanted you to bring back. If you made the mistake of bringing home something she did not tell you to, you would be beaten and made to sleep in the backyard whether it was winter or summer. Rain or hail, she would make you sleep in that old chicken coop that someone had built for her chickens. And if she was real mad at you, you had to sleep on the ground.

Mama had one of those ice machines that the people for whom Mr. Tex worked at a movie studio company had given to him. That machine made ice cubes and chipped ice. When I didn't do what Mama told me to do, I was made to sit in a tub of ice-cold water with ice cubes put in it. So you knew what was expected of you, and you had no choice. You did exactly what Mama told you to do if you valued your life.

Ronnie was one of the children who lived at the house with us. Mama had sent us to the grocery store so many times to steal meat. On one particular occasion she sent us to the store so many times for her party that would take place that night that the owner of the store and his son got suspicious and locked the doors so we could not get out of the store. He made us put all of the meat on the counter. Next he took the meat cleaver and threw it up in the air, and it would come down with the sharp end toward the ceiling. Then he would hit us on the back of the hand with the meat cleaver. He accidentally chopped off all four of Ronnie's fingers! I stopped stealing from that very day on no matter how many beatings I got. I was afraid to steal after that. Ronnie's fingers were on the counter, and he was holding his arm up screaming. The owner of the store did everything he could to stop the bleeding. He even started crying with us. He was yelling and screaming at his son to call the police. When the police got there, he rode with us to the hospital. We were in the back of the police car. We were just given back to Mama even after I told the police that Mama made us steal the meat. Nothing at all happened to her. The policeman talked to Mama outside of the door. When she came in she was smiling. My Mama had no remorse about what had happened to Ronnie's fingers. She said if Ronnie hadn't gotten caught, he would not have gotten his fingers chopped off. She began to laugh hysterically; "We will call him 'Nubby' from now on," she said. One day when we got up Ronnie was not there; I never saw him again; I do not know what happened to Ronnie. He was like one of our brothers.

Hot Mama and my brother 'Sonny' and I continued to find ways to sneak out of the house and get away from Mama hoping to fine my father so we could live with him. But the plainclothes cops and the policemen would always bring us back to Mama's home again. Even when Mama would beat us we would still run away whenever we got the chance. Once my brother 'Sonny' said, "We will sleep in the graveyard tonight because we would be safe there."

Restitution to the Church

One time, my brother 'Sonny' went into a Catholic Church in New York City and stole the little offering box where the money was kept in.

When I went to Hinesville, Georgia later in life I went to St. Stephen's Catholic Church and I gave the priests back the fifty-seven dollars my brother had taken. I told the priests that my brother had taken the money to feed me and my sister, 'Hot Mama.' The three of us had run away from home and my brother had no way to feed us and he needed enough money to buy the bus tickets to get to my father's house. But he never took me and 'Hot Mama' with him. He left us at the house of a lady who used to come and sleep with men at Mama's house. He told me and 'Hot Mama' that he would be back for us after he was gone for a week. The lady called Mama and she came with two men in a lady. We had to get in the back of the car and sit on the floor, and we were forced to have oral sex with the two men while Mama and the lady who was driving the car talked. I asked the priest if he could forgive my brother Sonny for stealing the money and if he could forgive me and 'Hot Mama' because we were with him. The priests gave me back the money. Even after I refused to take the money he said I had to because 'Jesus' (*"Yah'shua"*) had already forgiven me. He said, "Now you forgive you", and that is exactly what Father Jerry said to me. Every now and then I just go and sit by St. Stephen's Catholic Church. When I had the 'building The Heart of Christ was housed in' the Catholic Church would help me with the people I was serving. The priests have changed, but not the work that they do; they are still loving and caring for people with words that make you whole and not tear you down; words that say, "You are forgiven," always make a big difference in someone's life; it did in my life.

Working For Mama

Even when we were adults, my Mama had total control over all of her children except for 'Sonny' and myself. We were the two that got the most beatings because we did not submit, and that was a total 'no-no' in Mama's house eventually Sonny lost the battle. You had to do whatever you were told to do; you could not say no or why. You could only do what Mama said to do in any type of sexual act she demanded of you. She knew exactly what all of her clients' preferences was, and we had to be whatever they wanted us to be. Sometimes I would have to dress up like a grown lady, I mean, with stockings and high heels. Mama had bought them for me. She bought all of us high heels or the men who own a shoe store gave them to her for all of us, including my brothers, and the shoes really fit our feet. I remember the place where an old man fixed shoes one time or another. We all slept with him and he would bring Mama all kinds of high heels and pretty shoes for her. We would only get high heels if a client wanted to see us dressed up in them that way.

Barbara Jean

When my big sister Barbara Jean was a little girl, she had a lot of men who paid Mama to sleep with her. They would say, "She sure has some damn big, pretty legs." Although Barbara Jean was only 11 years old she was built like a woman, so Mr. Jesse always wanted to be with her until she was struck by a car. He resented that she had been struck by a car. I do not know what really happened to her. She would never talk about it to any of us, but if you tried questioning her she would cry and bang her head on the wall. Mama said Mr. Jesse had given her two bags of soda bottles. During that time people would cash soda bottles in for money. The more money you gave Mama, the better chance you had of not being hit or beaten, and Barbara Jean always thought of ways not to get hit or beaten. She always got money for Mama, no matter what she had to do to get it. After Barbara Jean came home from the hospital she still had glass glitter all over her body, even in her hair. She had to take lots of showers. After that she would sit and rock back and forth, back and forth, over and over again pulling out her hair and crying. She would bang her head against the wall for no reason at all. She would just rock back and forth, back and forth, and cry, even though nobody had touched her. She would bang her head into the wall and then start crying. She did this for the rest of her life; even as an adult she continued this behavior. She also developed a sleeping disorder. She would fall asleep even if she was standing up or eating. It did not matter what she was doing or where she was, she would fall asleep. One of the doctors that came to Mama's house to sleep with us said it was from stress from the accident. It wasn't due to the accident, it was due to Mama. She had destroyed my big sister's life by the time she was 14 years old. She was totally dehumanized by our Mama. She was killed later by her boyfriend, who stabbed her in the head because my Mama had told her to go out and make her some money. Her boyfriend had told her if she went out and prostituted herself again he would kill her. She was so afraid of Mama she did what she was told to do; she would do whatever Mama told her. He was waiting for her when she came in. The only thing he said to her was, "I told you what I would do to you." I was told she died right in front of Mama's doorway and Mama would not call the police; my big sister lay in that hallway for about six hours before the police were notified. Mama was in the house. She knew exactly what had happened to her daughter and she did nothing to save the life of my big sister Barbara Jean. I know this is bad to say, but I am glad my big sister is not hurting anymore. I believe she went home to be with "*Yah'shua*" the Messiah, I believe she is safe now, and no one can ever again hurt her or terrorize or torture her again. She will not be forced to use her body for sex. I believe she is in heaven now, waiting for all of us to see her again. She won't be banging her head or rocking back and forth, pulling out her hair and crying. She is completely healed in heaven, laughing and talking with angels and getting to know "*Yah'shua*" and "**Father Yah'uah**" *Elohim*; that's what I tell myself to ease my pain whenever I think about how much I love and miss her.

My Brother 'Sonny'

My brother 'Sonny" died of an overdose of drugs, but the truth is no amount of drugs or alcohol would take the anguish from his heart and soul. He was always afraid of having children. He thought he would treat them as we were treated, so he never had children of his own. There were children around him, but he was constantly afraid of them. He did not want to do anything inappropriate with them, so he would not let himself even be in a room by himself with anyone's children. He constantly had nightmares. He did not sleep well at night. While he was sleeping, he would jump up if he heard any type of sound and then he would start pacing the floor. I think he did that because whenever we were asleep Mama would come and beat us while we were in bed for something she said we had done earlier. I don't believe that was always true. I believe she liked seeing the terror on our faces. It gave her a sense of power over us. I don't sleep well at night, especially when I'm alone. I don't think any one of us does well at night. My brother 'Sonny' needed medication to get up, and when he got up he needed medication to lie down. When he would lie down, it would start all over again. Eventually he needed a pacemaker for his heart, but while he was yet young he had to have two big operations because of the stress that was on his heart. He said to me one day, "'Peewee,' living in Mama's house is like living in a war zone." His heart went bad because of stress. When we were little he would sometimes say to me, "'Peewee,' just let me do whatever Mama tells me to do to you so we won't get a beating." Mama made him have sex with one of her dogs. From that time on he hated animals. The last dog he had been good to was 'Midnight.' After that, every dog or cat that came into the house he would kill. Sometimes all of us would help him beat the dogs or cats to death. We would tie the animal up just like Mama would tie us up and we would help him beat that poor animal to death. With sticks and pipes.

Our Conduct

Now we innocent children had become monsters like what Mama was; we were looking for something or someone to prey on. We were killing things or destroying anything we knew Mama loved. I could not feel or tell right from wrong. It was just madness; yes, it was crazy homicidal madness coming out of us children. I was mad all the time, and I would fight all of Mama's clients. If Mama told me to do something with one of them I would pick a fight, so she got so many complaints about me. You weren't supposed to talk back to any adults. You only were supposed to do what you were told to do. You had to say to Mama, "Yes Ma'am" or "No Ma'am," and any man who spoke to you, you had to say "Yes Sir" or "No Sir."

You could not look Mama straight in the eye. If you did, you signed your own death warrant, or she would make you wish you were dead. I got hit in the head with hammers, was scorched with hot water, stabbed in the hand, forced to drink urine and thrown down the basement steps. Mama beat me with curtain rods, and burned me with the iron and her cigarettes. She beat me with switches and extension cords, hit me with boards, knocked me out with pipes, kicked me down flights of stairs, hung me up in the basement ceiling and put me on one leg.

If you cried you were told to shut up. We were not allowed to cry. At the same time if you did not cry, Mama would say, "You think you're bad, you're not going to cry, huh?" and when you did cry she would say, "Hush" and would beat you worse. After awhile I could not feel any type of pain. It was not like I'd say, "I'm not going to feel any pain today," I just didn't feel pain. I mean, I felt pain only when it got unbearable, but not like other people. I felt that initial hit; after that, nothing else. Most of the time I would go into laughing hysterically, even though I'm hurting something terrible and my brain stopped working properly. I know I'm hurting, but I would go into a place and I do not know how I got to that place. I could hold back the terror for awhile, until the pain got out of control; only then could I feel the terror of the pain.

Mama's Attempt to Control Me

Mr. Jesse was the biggest man we had ever seen. My sister, Gail Christine, was called 'Hot Mama.' When people would come to choose us, Mama would say, "Do you want to try my baby 'Hot Mama?'" Mr. Jesse paid Mama to have sex with 'Hot Mama.' When he did, she could not breathe properly and her ribs hurt her. So every time he would choose her, I would beg him to take me instead. He really preferred Barbara Jean but after she got hurt, he did not want her very often. Once he cut my upper thigh a little way from my vagina and he drank the blood from that place. When he tried to put his penis in my mouth, I bit it, and he threw me across the room into the wall. I bounced off the wall on to the floor. Mama wanted to kill me for doing that. She said, "You, #*&* #*." All of those famous curse words—she called me every last one of them. She said, "You are the dumbest child I have ever seen. You're the ugliest one of all the children in the house. You are the stupidest one I have ever seen and the stubbornness child in my house. From the day you were born I have hated you; nobody really wants to be with you, like they do Barbara Jean or any of the other children; they all really hate you and I hate you the most. Get the hell out of my face." These are my Mama's famous words, to me words of hatred and contempt. She was always displeased with me. I always made Mama mad; no matter what I did she was never pleased with me.

I was not trying to be stubborn; I was not trying to be dumb nor stupid nor ugly, not even rebellious. And I certainly was not trying to challenge Mama, nor was I trying to misbehave. I was not trying to be better than the other children; I really wanted to please Mama. I just wanted to stop her and the others from hurting me. I don't know what was worse: Mama trying to break me of my stubbornness or my trying to stop them from hurting me. I use the word stubbornness because I don't know what word to use for my actions. I knew I would get beaten but I still tried to stop Mama from hurting me. Mama always had a plan if you made her real mad, and I had pushed every button in the solar system of her very soul and in her universe she control everything. Her soul was mad at me and in Mama's world complete submission was demanded. I had broken the rules of her universe and Mama was waiting for the right opportunity to get rid of me. She still could make money off of me so it was not my time yet. I did not know when or how, but I knew Mama had a plan and it was well in motion. I could feel her hatred of me closing in on me; how people feel love. Is how I felt her hatred of me? I always wanted Mama to love me and my brothers and sisters; I know now she really could not. She was not capable of loving us. We meant nothing to her; all she cared about was money, her animals, and her clients. When she got up in the morning the first thing that Mama did was to give us one of her famous lessons on how to please her clients. Those were the things that Mama cared the most about—pleasing her clients. Her whole world revolved around making her clients happy. We were not even subhuman beings to Mama. At times I would make-believe she did love me and she was real good to us, but she never was. Not one day was our Mama ever good to any one of us. She would say or do something mean to us every single day that we lived in her house, just to make herself laugh at the way we responded to the harsh treatment. She would mock the expressions on our faces when she was hurting us, or she would make the sounds that we made when she was hitting us, or she would imitate the movement we did. I can hear her saying, "Please don't hit me, please, please don't hit me, Mama." She would stretch out that word "please" as long as she could, and then she would holler with laughter. Mama was mocking us and laughing all the way, tears running down her face laughing at us. The way we were in pain brought her great joy. She never felt sorry for anything she did to us. She always made us feel we caused her to behave that way.

'Midnight' the Dog

My brother 'Sonny' stole someone's cocker spaniel. I believe it was my sixth birthday. 'Sonny' brought the baby puppy dog home. He said, "'Peewee' this is your puppy dog. You give him a name." All of us were trying to name the baby puppy dog. 'Sonny' said, "We will call him 'Midnight,' okay 'Peewee'?" I said, "Okay, 'Sonny.'" I loved the name 'Midnight' because 'Midnight' was black, and 'Sonny' explained to me that 12 o'clock at night was midnight. The baby puppy dog was jet black with no white on him. His eyes were still shut tight. We all loved the baby puppy dog. For once we were like children. The baby puppy dog was so tiny that he fit in my hands. We had to feed him with a baby bottle. I carried him with me everywhere I went. He slept in the bed with me. He would tuck his head under my neck or under my shoulder, and we would go right to sleep. We did everything together, my baby puppy dog and me. He went everywhere with me. I wanted that baby puppy dog so badly that I would do anything to keep him. I did not give Mama any more trouble for months. I also didn't quarrel with any of Mama's clients. When I had to sleep with someone, 'Midnight' would wait by the door for me. He would not go and eat; he just sat there waiting for me to come out of the room no matter how long it took me. He would not move until I came out of the room as a child. 'Midnight' was my only joy and happiness, and the only thing that loved me besides my brother 'Sonny' and my sister 'Hot Mama.' I would talk to my dog but not to my brother and sister. I would listen a lot to 'Sonny' and 'Hot Mama.' The two of them had saved my life more than once; they always had to find ways to talk me down from saying no to something Mama had commanded us to do. 'Hot Mama' would have to reinforce in my head that I had to do whatever Mama said.

Mama's Vengeance

Whenever Mr. Jesse was ready to be with me, he would make me completely undress. He placed all of his things on a table. The things that he would eventually violate me with were on the table. Mama never said to him "you're hurting my children" or "this is not good for them." Sometimes she would watch every single thing that was done to us. Never once did she say that this is not part of the agreement and sometimes she would watch the abuse with a semi-smile of approval on her face. One day when I had to sleep with Mr. Jesse, he cut my ankle and drank the blood from it. When he cut me, I did not feel it. I was just mad that he cut me. Two days later my feet were hurting me, it had swollen up so big. When it happened, Mama grabbed a spider's web from the corner of the wall and placed it on the cut, and told me, "Now get out of my face." For two days I was steaming, and all I could think of was, "I am going to show him." I had no fear of him. I couldn't think about anything else except how to stop him. All I knew was that I was going to stop him. When he got undressed, he put his things on the table including an ice pick. I grabbed the ice pick, and stuck it in his hand. That made Mama mad once again.

She did not come and beat me in the middle of the night as she had done so many times before, so I thought she was not going to hurt me. What Mama did was to get me up early the next morning. She gave me a bath, brushed my teeth, put clean underwear on me and a can-can slip and a pretty pink dress with my white socks and my Buster Brown shoes that my father had bought for me. We called the slip that goes under your dress to make it stand out a can-can slip. The only time we got to wear the clothing our father brought for us was when he came or when we were going to one of Mama's clients' houses or offices. But this time Mama did not say we are going to see a client; she said, "We're going shopping." I thought Mama was not mad at all with me, but Mama knew how to play this game too well and I did not, and Mama always won. Mama and I got off the train at Hoyt and Shermerhorn st. Mama held my hand in her hand so gently, and every now and then she would look down and smile at me. We went shopping at the big department store called E. J. Korvette's. Mama said the only people that could afford to go shopping at E. J. Korvette's department store were people like her with lots of money. She said to me, "One day, 'Peewee,' you will buy yourself lots of pretty things too." Mama bought perfume, powder, earrings, pretty lingerie stockings and adult underwear, but she bought nothing for her children at all, just adult clothing and presents for her clients. I did not care if Mama did not buy us anything, I was just happy to be with my mama. Mama looked down and smiled at me. Her voice held so much excitement in it. She was happy and I was happy to be with her. It was just Mama and I. And every time Mama looked down at me and smiled, I would feel happy she was smiling at me. She was so beautiful. And Mama wanted to be with me and she was not hurting me, she was just happy to be shopping with me. I loved Mama so much that I was happy to be with her and I was happy that Mama was not mad at me. We walked and Mama would say from time to time, "How does this look on me, 'Peewee'?" Isn't this pretty? Someday you'll have your own things, won't you now?"

Then Mama took me to a dentist's office. It had a big dentist's chair in the middle of the room; to me it looked like just a room with a big chair in it. He said to Mama, "I will call you to let you know when to come and pick her up." He gave Mama some money, and Mama left me there. He undressed me and tied me to the chair face up. He tied the knots so tight around my wrists that they cut my skin. I was not sitting in the chair; I was spread out over the chair like a sheet. The ropes were so tight. They passed from the top of the chair to the bottom, then through the opening part of the chair. Then he tied one foot at one end of the rope and the other foot to the other end of the chair. Then he beat me with a whip from my head down to my feet, back up to my face. All over the front part of my body I was beaten. Blood was splattered everywhere, on the walls, on the floor, up on the ceiling, on the cabinet doors, and all over his white coat. I got hit so many times with that whip, and so many times in my face that he cut out a piece of my eyebrow. It is still missing today. Today I still have those same scars all over my body; when I dress up I have to wear jet-black stockings so I can hide the scars. When he untied me, I slid out of the chair through the opening at the bottom of the chair and onto the floor. I could not run, I could not move, and I could not holler anymore. My mind had gotten stuck. I could see myself looking through the eyes of a child again. He picked me up, put me back in the chair face down, and proceeded to have anal sex with me. Then he turned me around, got some tools, and began putting things into my mouth. Then he took a machine and began drilling my teeth. He never said a word at all to me but he made sounds like he was the one being hurt. I was tied back onto the chair. Everything I had to do, I did in that chair. He did not let me go to the bathroom, he did not give me any food or water or any medicine. He left me in that chair all night long, tied up in the dark, with nothing covering me except for my own blood all over me.

The next day he and a lady came in. She cleaned his office all around me, not saying a word to me. It was as though I was not even there. When she was ready to leave, she kissed him goodbye and said, "Enjoy your toy," and left. As a child I did not understand what she really meant. I was hoping he would play with his toys so he wouldn't hurt me anymore at the time I did not know I was the toy. I do not remember how many times that he beat me or how many times he had sex with me in every way you can imagine. I do not remember how many days I was there, but my mind was frozen. I could not even think at all. It was as though my mind was asleep. I could not feel or talk; I was just looking through the eyes of a child.

'Dissociation'

I'm going to explain what that means to me and tell you what it feels like. It is like I'm seeing things but like I'm looking through someone else's eyes. Those eyes are so frightened that they cannot think to run, so they just stand in place, watching every move you make, barely moving or breathing, just looking. You may have seen a child not respond when you tell him or her to do something. You may say he or she is just being stubborn, but they are not. They cannot think to do what you want them to do. Their minds get stuck. Even when you put their hands on the object to pick it up, they do not understand the command, so they do nothing but pull their hands back, stand still, and stare back at you. It gets especially intense when you use a lot of harsh words or screaming and cursing at them. They see you as a giant who has frightened them to death. Now total fear has taken over. They are certainly not being stubborn or disobedient; I think they get so confused, their brains stop working for a short time or longer. The whole time they're trying to think, you are screaming and yelling and hitting them so they cannot think to do what you want them to do, or move; they just stare at you so you think they are challenging you the truth is (they are not). So you begin to scream at the child more and more; you get angrier and angrier and they get more frightened. Usually those children are beaten severely or beaten to death. That's how it was for me.

My Visions

Ever since I was a child I have had all kinds of visions. My whole life I've seen things that other people could not see or hear, things like numbers, days, names of people and places, even words that were not common words for me to use or things I should not have known. Most of it I did not understand; I only would repeat what I heard. It was almost like watching a movie. When it would happen, I would not be afraid; I thought all people had visions. These visions came without my looking for them. If I would hear your voice or see a picture of you or lay my head on something of yours, I would know all kinds of things. Most of the time I hid from people so they could not ask me to tell them anything!

Mama used my 'gift' (or 'curse') to milk her clients dry. White and black people would come to see the little girl who could tell them things. I always thought it was a 'curse' because people expected so much from a child. Even today people treat me like I'm looking into a crystal ball and think that I can tell them anything they ask me about their life. I cannot. I can only tell them what I hear from the (Holy) Spirit of "**Father Yah'uah**," what He tells me. At that time I did not understand that it was a gift from Father Yah'uah.

Many people who have this type of 'gift' (or 'curse') have it from childhood, and they use it for the work of Satan. That is exactly what Mama encouraged in me. Lots of times I would hear things to say to the person but I would not say anything; I would tell them, "I cannot hear or see anything." If I did not say all kinds of good things to Mama and her clients, Mama and her clients would be mad at me, or I would be beaten. Even today as a 'Christian,' I am treated the same way when people want me to go beyond what I initially heard; they get mad at me, so most of the times I choose to say nothing. When I was little at Mama's house, I would get the beating of my life because I was messing up Mama's money. If I said to a lady that her husband was not cheating on her but she was cheating on him, I got beaten for telling the truth. When they would ask me something, I would say, "I cannot hear anything at all," but not because I had not heard anything; I just did not want to say the truth and get beaten, so I chose not to say anything.

I do not know my twin sister's name or if she was really my twin sister because so many children were always in and out of the house, but I know Mama said she was my twin sister. We were chosen to come out of the cage fence when two men paid Mama for us. We were put in the kitchen sink. There were people all over the place kissing and hugging one another and dancing. Loud music was playing, and people were having sex in front of us and in front of other people. Money was on the floor and on the table. They were playing all kinds of card games and shooting dice; I do not know the names of all of the card games they were playing. I thought they were having lots of fun because they were laughing so loud.

There were two baby bottles on the kitchen sink. My twin sister picked up one of the baby bottles and began sucking it. We were always hungry and thirsty. Then the two men began cursing at one another and began fighting. Then one of the men came to the kitchen sink and pushed my twin sister backwards and cut her stomach open. When I looked up, Mama was helping them hold her down. Her legs were still kicking. I tried to put the things back into her stomach. I thought she had swallowed a snake, or that she was so hungry she had eaten a snake, because of how things looked inside of her. I tried to put the blood back inside of her and the things that were coming down out of her. Her legs kicked slower and slower, and then stopped moving. Then they put her in a pillowcase. For a long time I could not touch any meat that had blood on it, even after I became a woman. I would get stuck, I couldn't move; sometimes I would just be staring at nothing. I could see people moving their lips, but I could not respond to them. I was seeing myself through the eyes of a child.

Mama's Legacy

I wonder sometimes, "How could **"Father Yah'uah"** *Elohim* give Mama Children for her to destroy them? He did not give us to her for that purpose. It was her choice to destroy us. She wanted everything that the world had to offer, even at the destruction of her own children's lives; we were nothing to her. When Mama became ill ~~sister's~~ she went to live at her sister's house. I asked her how she could have destroyed her own children's life. I asked Mama if she loved us; she said, "No, y'all meant nothing to me; I could spit out children a dime a dozen." I said to my Aunt Edna, "As long as Mama is living I will send you money every month to take care of her but I will never see her again." When my sister Gail Christine ('Hot Mama') called me to tell me my Mama had died, she asked if I was coming to the funeral and said she needed money to help bury Mama. This is what I said to her: I said "No" to my sister, 'Hot Mama.' I was not coming. I was not upset; I felt nothing. I felt like so many heavy weights had been lifted off of me. I was not happy and I certainly was not sad. I felt nothing except for the weights being lifted off of me. 'Hot Mama' said, "'Peewee,' no matter what Mama done to us she was still our mother." I said, "'Hot Mama,' I had no mother." My friend Margaret gave me the money with which to help bury my mama; to this day I do not know where in South Carolina my Mama's body is buried. I don't know how I am able to forgive Mama. To this day I am able to shut completely down. It happens whenever I am stressed. I shut all feelings off; they just go away. Anything concerning Mama or anything bad—my mind simply does it—I have to force myself to remember things that happened in Mama's house, not so that I can be angry with her, just so I can remember my sisters and brothers. Sometimes I forget they ever existed; for months or even years I will not remember one of them, then memories start coming back like a flood. At those times it is hard for me to even associate with people. Had it not been for 'The Heart of Christ Ministry' and the church, I don't know what would've happened to me. Had it not been for my children and nephew Kincade Douglas and Margaret Autry, I know I would not have been here today. 'Papa' Curt and his wife, Gretchen, and Ronald Ellyson, and Ms. Debbie all of them reinforced in me the truth that I am a human being I am somebody special and someone unique. They affirmed that the world is a better place because I'm in it, that I am created in the 'image' of **"Father Yah'uah"** *Elohim*, that I have been called and chosen by *"Yah'shua"* the Messiah, and that he loves me just as much as he loves the rest of the world.

Perversity and 'Jesus'

Memories have a way of coming out when they want to. They are screaming to be heard, so they play a game like hide and seek. When you are trying to seek them, they are trying to hide because you have buried them; so deeply inside of you they are the hideous memories that you do not want to seek. Most of the times they find you at the wrong time in the wrong place, then you have to work harder to hide them again; yes, it is a game like hide and seek that your mind plays with you to keep you safe from harming you are someone else. However when **"Father Yah'uah"** *Elohim* seeks you there's nowhere to hide these memories he wants you to hand them over to him so he can heal you. When He calls you, then you will come and lay down all of the hidden disgusting memories that are hidden deep down inside of you. You will put them at His son Yah'shua the Messiah feet at the foot of his cross and he will bear the sins that were committed against you every hurt in pain in your heart becomes his. On His altar you can lay down all of the 'monsters:' the beatings, the lying, stealing, the drugs or lifestyles, the pain, the shame, the hate and the rape. You now have a place to lay down death and destruction, and that place is at the feet of "*Yah'shua*" the Messiah. He will breathe new life into your nostrils; *Yah'shua*" will make you one with **"Father Yah'uah"** and himself.

I remember at one time I could not even say the name of 'Jesus Christ' because of what Mama had let one of her clients do to me. He was a preacher. He would get there early and would read his Bible until 12 o'clock. Then he would sit at the table and begin to gamble with the people. Did he think by using someone else's money that he wasn't doing something wrong with us? What was this 'man of God' thinking? When he would win, he would pick a child he wanted to be with that night. Whenever he had sex with me, I had to say, "thank you, 'Jesus'". He would say that name over and over, so to me 'Jesus' was the bad guy. I really did not know who his 'Jesus' was. I thought he was his friend or someone in his family like his brother. We weren't taught anything about 'God' or 'Jesus Christ.' At no time at all did Mama teach us how to pray or to whom to pray to. She said she was our 'god.'

The Twenty-Third Psalm

My sister, 'Hot Mama' (Gail Christine), taught me how to say the 23rd Psalm. She said, "'Peewee,' whenever you are afraid, just say this prayer." I say, "'Hot Mama,' I just cannot remember the words." She said "Say what I say." So she taught me the 23rd Psalm just before she left to go live with Nellie Rachel. They called Nellie Rachel 'Billy.' She had a girl who lived with her but she wanted 'Hot Mama.' So the girl came to live with us, and my sister went to live with Nellie Rachel. I cried so much because I missed 'Hot Mama.' Her and my brother Sonny was the only ones who could talk me down when I got into trouble. She would always say, "'Peewee' do-not think about it, just do it when she came to visit us, she would say, "'Peewee,' just dance in your head like Fred Astaire and Ginger Rogers, or think about James Cagney." James Cagney was our favorite actor. He was not afraid of anybody, and he could dance too. We must have seen every picture James Cagney and Fred Astaire and Ginger Rogers played in. She said, "'Peewee,' you have to be strong for all of us." So she would tell me to say the 23rd Psalm with her. All the time she would say, "Repeat after me, 'Peewee,' 'The LORD' is my shepherd; I shall not want. He makes me to lie down in green pastures; He leads me beside the still waters. He restores my soul: He leads me in the path of righteousness for His name's sake. Yea though I walk through the valley of the shadow of death, I will fear no evil; for you' are with me; your rod and your staff they comfort me. You prepare a table before me in the presence of my enemies; you' anoint my head with oil; my cup runs over. Surely goodness and mercy shall follow me all the days of my life; and I will dwell in the house of 'The LORD' forever." 'Hot Mama' said, "'Peewee,' this prayer will keep you at all times."

The prayer did not mean anything to me. I had repeated it lots of times with my sister. She had told me 'God' could do anything. I thought, and then I said, 'God' did not know Mama, and if 'God' did, he would be afraid of Mama! By no means was I trying to be smart with my younger sister; I was just stating what I believed at that time. If He did know Mama, why didn't He stop her from hurting us? So that made me think He was afraid of her too. I did not understand the power of 'God.' I don't believe 'Hot Mama' knew 'God;' she just believed a story an old lady told her, so she told it to me, I didn't think it was true how could words save you? Now I know because they belong to God who is Father Yah,uah.

Death of 'Midnight'

I am going to tell you how 'Midnight' died. Mama wanted me to let 'Midnight' have anal sex with me. I would not let him get close to me. Every time 'Midnight' came close to me, I would kick him so he sat and looked at us. She would call him, and I would say, "Sit!" When he saw I was struggling to get away from Mama, he started growling at her. He bit her legs and hands and then he bit Mama all over. He would bite anyone who was trying to hurt me, even Mama. Her hand was bleeding. He bit her to the bone you could see the pink meat. Mama let me go. She took care of her hand to stop the bleeding. Then she got some ground beef from the fridge she let the meat become unfrozen. She got two Coca-Cola bottles, put them in a sock and beat them with a rolling pin until they were fine glass. The glass looked like the glass that was all over Barbara Jean when she came home from the hospital. Mama cooked the meat, mixed it with the glass and put it down between the two doors where the food for 'Midnight' was kept. As long as Mama stood by the door, he would not go near the food. When she went to her room, 'Midnight' ate the food. 'Midnight' started throwing up blood, and blood was coming from his rectum. He was turning around and scratching himself against the floor and door where he was kept, and he would howl like a wounded animal. He would bite me every time I tried to pick him up. Before that day he had never bitten me. I wanted 'God' to help 'Midnight.' I wanted somebody to give 'Midnight' some kind of help so I repeated the

23rd Psalm, and I asked 'Jesus', "Please, please 'Jesus', please 'God', save my dog." But 'Midnight' got worse so I asked 'God' to let him die so he wouldn't hurt no more. I opened the door where 'Midnight' was kept. He came to me; I stooped down. He put his paws on my shoulders, he tucked his head under my chin and he died. I sat there for a long time. I was not crying just holding my dog. My brother 'Sonny' had to tear him out of my arms. 'Midnight' had become cold and as stiff as a board but I would not let him go.

My Retaliation

Everything that had ever been done to me was rushing through my body. Years of abuse were kicking in. I was hollering but not making a sound. I was screaming but not making a sound. I was crying but not shedding a tear. I was dying but not dead. I kept repeating the 23rd Psalm over and over again. Where was 'God', **"Father Yah'uah"** *Elohim*? He was there in the 23rd Psalm. After that I stopped talking for a long time. I was seeing everything through the eyes of a child, and everything I was told to do I did. Mama had no problems out of me whatsoever. You could see on her face the look of victory. Mama had won; she had broken me. She had taken every ounce of innocence out of me. All you could see was the 'monster' that dwelled inside of me. When 'Hot Mama' would come, she would sit and rock me in her arms or lie in the bed next to me and just cry with me, rocking me and telling me, "'Peewee,' you just keep saying the 23rd Psalm." For months Mama had total peace from me: no complaints from her clients and no complaints from anyone. Even when I had to fight one of the other children for that plate of food, I would fight them and win the fight and leave the plates of food. I was alive. Yet I was as if dead and I felt nothing. And I wanted nothing; I was just staring at them through those childlike eyes. I wasn't frightened, and I wasn't afraid of any of them. I felt totally nothingness; I could see them and hear them but I felt like someone else was watching them and waiting for the right opportunity to get them all back. There was no talking in my head.

My baby sister Adrian, who we called 'Koochie Mama,' had to sleep with Mr. Tom. He drove one of those big trucks. He did not come to Mama's house often. There was some type of commotion, and he beat 'Koochie Mama' in her face. Her face swelled up and her eyes turned black and blue it was completely red inside. When I saw her I never asked her what had happened; I never said a word to anyone. I walked into the kitchen and got a knife and jumped on him like a cat does and stabbed him. I wrapped my legs around the upper part of his body and stabbed him in his shoulder blade; he dropped to his knees. The adults wrestled the knife from me. All I kept thinking was, "I am going to stop him;" he went down to his knees. I had seen so many people get drunk and start fighting one another, then shooting or stabbing each other. Two other men took him from the house; I do not know where they took him. The other people in the house were leading me from the room that it had happened in. I kept looking over my shoulder to see if he was going to come back into the house and I was thinking I had to get him first. Mama just stared at me with so much anger in her eyes. I couldn't see anybody; I couldn't feel anybody. All the people who would come to Mama's house stopped coming. They were afraid of the tiny one in the house. They would say, "Barbara, you got to get rid of 'Peewee.' She is going to kill somebody or hurt them real bad. We could not hold that child. Barbara to look at that child was like looking at Satan; he was in that child. Barbara, she's going to ruin your business if you don't get rid of her." They were worried about me hurting one of them! Why weren't they thinking about them hurting one of us? The animals that were in Mama's house got treated better than we were. Mama never put one hand on them or let anyone else hurt her animals, but she let them do all kinds of things to us. As I said, Mama had a plan for me, and it was well in motion.

Mama's Houses

We were still living at 109 W. 84th St., apartment 2B. It is amazing that I have not remembered or thought about that apartment for a number of years. I had to be at least six or seven years old. I am now 61 years old. But I remember it because when people would come for the first time and knock on the door, they would say, "Is this apartment 2B?" Mama would say, "I got whatever you are looking for. If I don't have it, I will get it for you." And Mama would get it for them. We were in the daily newspaper because the apartments at 109 W. 84th St. were infested with rats and mice. They lived side by side with us children. They would have their baby's right next to us. We were not afraid of them, and they weren't afraid of us.

Mama had another house we lived in. The house at 178 Carlton Avenue, in Brooklyn New York was her second house. The house was very beautiful. It had chandeliers and wood floors, throw rugs, couches and chairs in all the bedrooms, and all kinds of beautiful furniture. Mr. Tex was her boyfriend at that particular time. He worked for a movie company, and they would give him a lot of the props that he would make for them and lots of furniture, so Mama's second house looked like a mansion. It had an upstairs and a downstairs and a small house attached to it. It had a fire escape, it had a basement, and it had a laundry room. It also had a chicken coop in the back yard and a big kitchen. We had to keep that house clean. We had to scrub the baseboard with a toothbrush and mop and wax the floor on our hands and knees, and about four in the morning we had to clean the chandeliers. Every Saturday morning Mama would say, "Get the hell up now # *& # @. It is 4 o'clock in the morning and y'all still got your @ #*@ in the bed. Get the hell up now!" We were Mama's slaves.

Mama's Influence with Authorities

These are the people that came to Mama's house to sleep with her children: the bus drivers, the police officers, cabdrivers, teachers, preachers, attorneys, judges, firemen, doctors, people from the studio in the movie studio Mr. Tex worked for and the truant officer from the school. Mama never was prosecuted, never put in jail or never even arrested. When her children would talk in the court, we were punished. So to this day it is difficult for me to trust people in any authority. I saw the wickedness they can do and no one put a hand on them. If you have a title you can get away with just about anything as long as you have the money to go with that title. My mama's title was "I got what you want, but if I don't have it I will get it for you." It opened all kinds of doors for her. I had run away so many times, and I would fight so many children and teachers at the school that the courts put me in an all-girls detention home for bad girls. I was bad.

My Defense of Barbara Jean

Here are some of the bad things that I did. My sister Barbara Jean had to hold 'Hot Mama's and my hand while she took me to school the short time that we did go. She would say, "Hurry up, 'Peewee,' or we'll be late." She would stop at the candy store and go in the back room with a man. When she came out, she would have a big bag of candy and money for Mama. Barbara Jean did this every day we went to that school. One day some big girls were fighting Barbara Jean. She was 11 years old she may have been younger I'm not sure and I was six or seven years old. They were chasing her and she let go of my hand. They caught my big sister. She rolled up like a ball on the ground. They were kicking her, and stomping her, punching her, and hitting her. She balled up and covered her face like she did when Mama was beating her. My sister 'Hot Mama' ran home to get my Mama. I started fighting everything that was moving. I bit one of the girls in her throat. I kicked and stomped some of the girls. I stomped one girl's eyeball out of her head. The adults came to stop the fight. They hitting me and I was hitting them back. I was biting them and fighting them just like our dogs would or like Mama beat us. By the time Mama got there, the police were called and everything was over. Mama's only concern was if Barbara Jean got hurt, she couldn't go out with one of her clients. My sister Barbara Jean brought in the most money for Mama. They liked her to look real pretty when they took her out; that was Mama's only concern. I remember one of the police officers saying,

"Damn, I don't want to get in a fight with that little thing." They handcuffed me and began bopping me on my head. I was thinking if I can get out of those hand cups I would pop him on his head. They put me out of school but the courts did not lock me up because all the girls were in fourth and fifth grade, and I was just in first grade or kindergarten I'm not sure of which one. From that day on none of the children would touch any of my sisters and brothers. If someone started a fight with one of them, they knew they had me and the rest of us to fight. We were not afraid to fight, because we always had to fight one another. And we were used to being beaten, so the children did not stand a chance. Nobody wanted to fight with one of us, especially 'Sonny' or myself or 'Hot Mama.' It was almost like fighting with a crazy adult or children with adult strength. My sister Hot Mama was shorter than I and she was very tiny and very deadly she had the worst temper of all of us she would try to get away from you but when you left her no choice. It was no stopping her it took a while to get her to that place but I saw the monster that had been created in her but she loved me and I loved her as a child I did not see the monster inside of her it was when we became old that I could see the hatred illuminating out of us. The next bad thing I did happened when one of the teachers in my school, who was one of Mama's clients, asked me to do some sexual things with her at the school. When I refused, she gave me a note to give to Mama. When I got home I gave the note to Mama. Mama asked me for my book bag. When she opened it, it had all kind of toys in it. Mama said, "You don't want to listen to anyone at that school? Ha, you think you're grown?" I did not think I was grown, I did not know how those toys got in the book bag, and I told Mama so, but she beat me anyway. The next day when I went back to school, my teacher started bragging how she had made me get a beating. The next day the teacher was taking the class downstairs to the auditorium. I was supposed to be in the middle of the line but I got all the way to the back and stayed at the top of the stairs. When she took the class to the auditorium and saw I was missing, she came back for me. I had seen her do that with other children so I waited there for her to come for me. She said, "Stand right there." I was standing right there waiting for her to get closer. She started up the stairs towards me. I waited for her to get close to me. When she did, I pushed her down the steps just like Mama had done to me. Her leg went in back of her. She was a heavyset lady. She broke her leg and wrists. She was out of school for a couple of days. They put me out for a couple of weeks. She told the principal I was playing around at the top of the stairs when I should have been in the auditorium with the rest of my classmates that it was an accident but it was not an accident I did it on purpose. And she knew it because she told Mama the true.

Mrs. Novacar, and the Substitute Teacher

When they let me come back in school, I was put in a class with older children who were older than me. My teacher at that time was Ms. Novacar, who was John F. Kennedy's aunt. She taught the fourth grade. They put me there because no one else would take me and there classroom. The teachers were all afraid of me. They were afraid to even let me play with the other children because I would beat them at the drop of a hat. But Ms. Novacar was different. She knew something was going on at home but she did not know what was going on. She tried asking me, but Mama had warned me not to tell anybody anything that was going on at her house. She said. "I'll kill you as dead as a doornail if you do, if you tell anybody what goes on in my house." And I knew Mama meant it. Ms. Novacar told our class that John F. Kennedy was her nephew, and he was running for Senate. It would be years later that I would meet John F. Kennedy. Ms. Novacar would always bring me a sandwich and cookies. Even though I could not read and write she still let me stay in her class.

One day she got sick, and we had to have a substitute teacher. The substitute teacher said to me, "You have dirty clothing on, and you have a dirty neck." I have a birthmark on my neck, and even now my friends will say that it turns black at times. During strawberry season it even turns red sometimes. My daughter has the same mark on her arm. My son had it on his head, and my youngest child has that same mark on the lower part of his body. The children began laughing and calling me names like 'dirty neck bones neck.' Then the substitute teacher called me in front of the whole class and made me stand in a corner. I had not done anything wrong yet. Then she allowed another child to pick on me by calling me names. When I asked to go to the bathroom, she said, "No," she said that I only wanted to go to the bathroom so I could get away from the other children. That was the last straw. A boy was sweeping the floor, he was innocent but I had to use him. So I snatched the broom from him. I knew it would start a fight, and I knew it was a no-win situation for him. He wasn't the target of my anger. The teacher was, but I had to use him anyway so I put the fight in motion. He tried to take the broom back from me, but he couldn't; I hit him with it. When the teacher came over, I began hitting her and biting and beating her with the broom. I hit her with chairs, anything I could get my hands on. There was not a soul in that room but me and the substitute teacher. The children ran screaming and hollering out of the classroom. She was screaming for her life, and it was in my hands. I was beating her for everyone who had ever beaten me. Then some of the men teachers came into the room and tackled me to the floor. That was the end of school for me. The school was PS Nine, I believe. No, I know it was PS Nine.

Reform Schools

After the fight I was sent to Hudson Reform School for bad girls. I must admit I was a handful, but there were no adults that stopped people from doing things to me so I protect me. I was in Hudson for a while, and then I was sent to Manida Juvenile Center for girls. I was sent to another reform school for girls in the Bronx. After I had been locked up for a couple of year I heard some of the counselors talking about me going to court and then going home. Fear gripped me; I couldn't think straight. I did not have a plan but I did not want to go home. I was safe from Mama here, and I did not get many beatings. The only beatings I got were when I lost a fight, and I did not lose many of those, even though some of the girls were older than I was. Most of the beatings were given by me! I was frightened for the first time again I was not going home no matter what, I stopped talking. The girls thought that I was planning on doing something to somebody; I was just scared of going home to Mama's house. One of the older girls asked me what was wrong, so I told her I did not want to go home. She said, "If you fight the social worker or the counselor you will go to Creedmoor State Hospital." I did not know what Creedmoor State Hospital was, but I knew anywhere would be better than going home to Mama. I knew that I would have food to eat, I would not have to sleep with anyone, and I would be safe from Mama. So when the social worker came to do an evaluation I picked a fight. They had to call the men from the boys' side. I even did battle with the men. One of them punched me so hard in my stomach that my food flew up on him. I still did not stop fighting; them I felt like I was fighting for my life and I was not about to lose this battle. I knew if I went home that Mama would eventually kill me I had to do everything that came into my mind to save me. It was very hard to beat them because they had on padded clothing. It was one of me against a small army of them; there were about eight of them. It was a no-win situation but I had to start that fight to save my life, and I had put everything I had in this fight to be sure of my safety plus I had been beaten worse than this. Being sent home to Mama would have been worse.

Creedmoor State Hospital was a mental hospital was a mental institution which I didn't know at the time, but it was still better than going home to Mama they would keep me safe from Mama, there they kept me so drugged up that all I did was sleep. I did not have the strength to stand up, let alone fight anybody. I was always somewhere asleep, on the floor, under the bed, and in the shower. I lost so much weight that I was sent to the infirmary. They had to cut back on my medication.

Mama's Visit

During the first three years I was locked up I did not have one single visitor. But the whole time I still did not want to go home. I was safe in there. It was the court that ordered Mama to visit me I did not want her to come. When I saw her, I did not know who she was. When I had left home she was very small and thin; when I saw her again she was very big and heavyset. That day the counselors and social workers were just happy, and they were good to me. They gave me new clothes and shoes to put on. The dress was black with a white shirt under it. I had white socks on and a white bow in my hair. They said, "You look so pretty." At that time I had never been told I was pretty it would be only the second time I would hear those words in my life. I had been called ugly by Mama all of my life. She said, "You are the ugliest child I have." I never liked looking into mirrors. Even today I do not like to see my face in a mirror. They walked me down the hall, and the social worker kept saying to me, "We have a big surprise for you. You're going to be so happy." I thought it was going to be some type of birthday party for me. Other girls had birthday parties in that room but I hadn't, so I thought it was a birthday party for me. All I saw was a heavyset lady who was standing there. The social worker backed out of the room, so it was just me and the heavyset lady. She didn't say a word to me so I didn't say anything to her. She stared at me so I stared at her for awhile. Then she realized I did not know who she was so she said, "'Peewee.'" When I heard her voice, I opened the door and ran. The social worker grabbed me by my clothing pushed me back in the room by pulling my clothing. She said, "Where are you going Gloria?" I said I wanted to go back to the ward. I was thinking that I did not want to go anywhere with Mama. I couldn't talk; I couldn't say a word. She pushed me back into the room, and I pushed out of the room. Then she lifted me from the floor, and Mama grabbed hold of me and said, "'Peewee' what's wrong with you? You know who I am." I knew too well who she was. She was Mama. The court made her come one more time. Then she took me home.

My Foster Family

A Catholic Church that Mama was milking dry had given her so much money and so much food and clothing for her children whom they had not seen, that they sent a Catholic priest to the house to visit Mama. He told Mama to let us go to a camp program that the church was sponsoring when the summer came. If she did not, the church could no longer help her. She wanted all she could trick them out of so that she could give the things to her lady clients for their children, while we were sitting in a fenced cage with out clothing. I can still hear Mama's friends laughing and giggling as they rummaged through the things that were meant for us.

When summer came I went to live in Mannheim, Pennsylvania. I stayed with a white family that had three children of their own. Their oldest daughter's name was Judy. Judy was in a wheelchair. Her parents said she had soft bones. Judy's hair was blonde. She had blue eyes and a pretty smile. She couldn't talk, and she wore glasses. They had two sons. I cannot remember the two boys' names or the name of the mother and father. My first night there, they said to take a bath and go to bed. After I took my bath I went into their bedroom and got in their bed naked. They were shocked they wrapped me in the bed covering and asked me why I did that. I told them so they could do it to me. So they asked me all kind of questions, and I told them the truth. From that day on they did all that they could to keep me. But the court said no.

These people were the only ones in my life who wanted me for something other than sex. Judy's mother would read to me, and she gave me coloring books, crayons and reading books.

The church that they went to did not want me to attend I believe it was because I was black there were no other black people in that church I did not know at that time that, that was the reason I figured it out once I got older. But Sunday morning after Judy's mother had got me dressed we all went to the church. When we got to the church, Judy's father picked me up and walked through the doors with me in his arms. He sat down in the first row and introduced me as his other daughter, Gloria. Being in this family was one of the happiest times of my entire childhood. Judy's mother was so good to me, and her father was too, and I loved her two brothers. I was so happy living in their house that I wished I could live with them forever. This was a blessing from "**Father Yah'uah**" *Elohim* but I did not know that He was in that family that loved me so that I could have some happiness. I have tried to find them but I could not because I could only remember Judy's name and not their last name.

Buried in the Basement

When I had to go home, I took the books with me. Mama went through all of my things but I had dropped the books in between the two doors when the Catholic priests took me home because Mama had not come to pick me up. When I went upstairs where my brothers and sisters were, I hid the books from Mama. A couple of days later I gave the books and coloring books and crayons to my brothers and sisters. I could not read but I pretended I was reading. I had memorized the stories Judy's mother had read to me. Mama found out about our books and crayons so she built a fire in the back yard and burned our books. I was so mad that I went in her room, got her sweater and her shoes and threw them in the fire right in front of her face. What was I thinking? Had I really lost my mind? Mama picked me up. She threw me down the cellar steps. I was unconscious. She threw water on me until I woke up. She made all of my brothers and sisters and I dig a hole in the basement. She made me get in a box. I was fighting my brothers and sisters so that they could not put me in the box. My brother 'Sonny' was lying on top of me and said, "'Peewee', stop fighting us. I will come and get you out of the box." Then Mama nailed the box shut. She made my brothers and sisters put the box in the hole in the basement floor. They had to cover it up with dirt from the basement floor. Then she left the house for a long time. As soon as she left, 'Sonny,' Barbara Jean, 'Hot Mama,' and Deborah dug me out of that hole. Was the 'Holy Spirit' of *Elohim* guiding them? I think so! How could four small children using only their bare hands dig me out of the hole in the basement that took all 20 children to dig? It had to be the 'Holy Spirit' of *Elohim* somehow guiding my 4 brothers and sisters.

'Sonny' kept me upstairs so Mama couldn't see me. He stole food from Mama and from stores to feed me. He put a bucket upstairs for me to use and would go and empty it out. He would wet the end of a towel and wash me up. He would put food in his mouth, chew it up and feed it to me. He would hold my nose until I swallowed. I had got stuck again. I could see him, I could hear him, but I could not respond to him. I was seeing myself through the eyes of a child. Though I was still around, I was dead inside, and my mind was not there. When Mama found out my brother had me hidden upstairs while he went out scrounging and stealing food for us, she came upstairs and found me. She took me down stairs to the basement. She tied me up to the ceiling. She put fishhooks through my vagina. The weight of my body caused my vagina lips to split. It would be years later before a doctor in Hinesville, Georgia would repair the damage done to me. Mama sat quietly in a corner, not saying a word after struggling to hang me up on the basement ceiling. When my brother came back and could not find me he went straight to the basement. When he saw Mama, he begged Mama for my life. He was looking up at me; tears were streaming down his face. He said, "Mama, I would do anything for you; anything you tell me to do I will do. Please Mama; don't kill 'Peewee.'" My mama told my brother to break into a jewelry store and he did; he paid for my life with the jewelry he stole. He gave all of the jewelry to Mama. He knew he would have to break into more jewelry stores before he was finished paying for my life. If Darlus had not bought me from Mama it would be a matter of time before she would get rid of me permanently. My brother 'Sonny' knew Mama was well capable of getting rid of me forever and she would have no remorse about it. I was just another problem to her; I was something she would have to get rid of so her business could grow and her clients would be happy once again.

Elbe Darlus Campbell

A couple of weeks later Elbe Darlus Campbell paid Mama $500 for me. He would be the father of my oldest two children. We called him 'Cherokee' or Big Jack. Darlus was one of Mama's regular clients. They would always drink together. He would get drunk and she would steal his money after he would go to sleep with one of us. He had slept with every girl in that house including my mama. That is how I became his property.

I was one month from turning 13 years old when I was sold to Darlus. You could have looked at me and seen I was a little girl; I did not even look to be 12 years old, I looked much younger than 12. I did not look like a grown lady. I was not quite 4 feet tall. (Even now at 61 years old, I only stand 5 feet tall.) I had not developed a woman's body or a woman's sounding voice, and I had no breasts; at twelve I looked to be about eight years old. Darlus beat me all the time because I was so clumsy. I think I was scared most of the time. He would sometimes just beat me for fun in front of his girlfriend's when I could not follow one of his commands properly. He would bring other women to the house to have sex with him while I sat on the floor playing with a teapot and cups and saucers, and sometimes a baby doll he had given to me. He would let his friends sleep with me. I had to wash the women's panties, scratch their heads make them sandwiches, and bring them beer; go to the store, straighten or curl their hair, and rub lotion on their legs before they were ready to leave. I do not know why he bought me; I think he just wanted me as his property, because it sure was not love; I was something to boast about to his friends. Everything this man did to me hurt me. I cannot think of one happy day I had with him—not one.

'June Bug'

The only joy I had was when Darlus' nephew, Kincade Douglas—we called him 'June Bug'—he came to his uncle's house. He would come by the house to see his grandmother. I am five years older than he is. He would talk to me and would read to me. He would tell me what he did in school all day. He would answer all of my questions, and I had lots of them, but he would always give me an answer. When Darlus would get drunk and go to sleep, 'June Bug' would sneak me out of the house and walk me around the streets of Brooklyn, New York. He would tell me about everything I saw. "Even the stars," he said, "all stars have names." He would teach me the names of the streets. He also taught me how to ride the subway and how to recognize all of the stop signs by name. I could not read them. But I could recognize what each stop sign looked like and the things that were around them, so the things I saw at those stops were fixed in my mind. He would tell me, "Don't let anyone tell you that you are stupid or dumb. One day you will get away from Darlus and go to school like everybody else. In the meantime I'll keep teaching you. He would say when I grow up, I will protect you." I was so afraid of Darlus. I thought he would wake up and be mad at me for being out of the house and talking with 'June Bug,' so I could not remember the words he was teaching me. I was trying to listen; I was trying to learn to write my name. But I was so full of fear I couldn't always remember the words that 'June Bug' was trying to teach me. I could only remember how things looked. "June Bug' was always so full of hope. He always found a way to make me laugh, and even when I was mad with him he still found ways to make me happy. Even today he is the same way—he always tries to make me laugh. One of my friends once said, "When 'June Bug' is talking to you, you seem to be a different person," I knew I seem different. I can still hear the hope in his voice. He is still protecting me from being hurt; he always acts like he's my older brother who has to make sure I am all right. When my children said or do something wrong to make me feel bad he always wanted to tell them how hard I had it and how I struggled to make the best decisions I could for them; or he wanted to let my children know what my life was like. But I never would allow him to tell them. I was just happy he loved my children. He is a cousin to my Monique and Darlus. But because he is so much older than they are they have always called him 'Uncle June.' I'm most proud of how he loves my youngest son Lesroy who is not his cousin; because Lesroy's father was different from Monique's and Darlus' father, 'June Bug' has loved all three of my children and has not made Lesroy feel like he was any different. From his sister and brother all of their lives their 'Uncle June' has been there for them. One time I said to him, "I'm so jealous of the way Lesroy gets to go everywhere with you, but I and Monique do not." 'June Bug' has always protected me from his uncle; he hated the way he treated me. The innocence and purity of our relationship is what kept me going in those days. The Spirit of Father Yah'uah *Elohim* was there again, but I wasn't aware of it Father Yah'uah was helping me through June bug. He was helping Kincade Douglas protect me from Darlus the best he could do for an eight-year-old boy. That's how old 'June Bug' was when I first met him.

Life With Darlus

Darlus lived in the house with his mother. She had seen her son beating me lots of times, and the next day I would be up and moving around as though nothing had ever happened, even though I would be swollen and black and blue. She would fuss at him about beating me, but whenever I would call the police, she would be mad at me. He would beat her at times, but she loved her son in if she had to have him arrested she would bail him out the next day.

My Daughter Monique

At 17 years of age I was pregnant with my first child, Monique. 'June Bug' had to explain to me about babies and what to expect. I knew women had babies; I just did not know the process. Darlus was not with me during my pregnancy. He had moved in with another woman. When he came home during my last month, he put me out of his mother's house. His mother came and got me I was at his sister 'Flo's house. When I went into labor, I had no concept I was in labor. I thought I was hungry so I went into the kitchen and begin eating strawberry ice cream. But I kept feeling the pushing, so I went to Darlus' mother. "Susie," I told her, "something is wrong." I was on the way to the hospital in an ambulance when Monique was born. She weighed in at 4 pounds 13 ounces. Monique was so beautiful. She had a head full of curly black hair like my father and she was born looking white in about two years later she turned the complexion of her father. Darlus didn't see Monique until she was two weeks old.

Darlus' mother Susie took care of my baby. I was afraid of my baby, especially to see her naked. I could not change her Pamper or bathe her. Her grandmother Susie Campbell had to do that for me. I was okay with feeding her, but anything to do with seeing her naked I was afraid of. Darlus' whole family loved her. I knew she was my baby but I couldn't feel the love a mother was supposed to have for their child. I did not want anyone to hurt her, and I did not hurt her, but I knew the things Mama had done to us, and I was afraid I might do them to my children.

My daughter looked like an 'angel. 'I thought to myself, "How could something so beautiful come out of me?" I would look at her for hours and think, "What a wonderful gift from 'God' Father Yah'uah has blessed me with this baby girl." The first thing I did was to go to a Catholic church. By the door there was a thing on the wall. I do not know what it is called but water is in it. I had seen it on television how the people, when they would go inside of the church, would make the sign of the cross on themselves and say, "Father forgive me, I have sinned, in the name of the Father, the Son and the Holy Ghost." Sometimes they would say, "Virgin Mary, pray for me," so I said it too; I did the same thing to my new baby I wanted God Father Yah'uah to blessed her. But I didn't have a clue what it was all about but I knew that in all of the pictures I had seen on television about 'Jesus Christ' and 'God,' people would pray for forgiveness, and then touch the water, blessing themselves with it. There was one picture that I really loved and I cried about it. It was called "The Boy Who Made 'Jesus' Come off the 'Cross'." I loved that movie picture so much.

But as beautiful as my daughter was, I was afraid of her and angry because the man who gave her to me had not been good to me at all. I was forced to have all kinds of crazy sex with him. I was held out the window by my neck, beaten constantly, put out of the house (sometimes without clothing), and forced to sleep with his friends. How could I love him? The biggest problem was that I was his property, not even a human being. I had no rights at all, and I had no place to go. Whenever he wanted me back at his house, I could not say "I won't go in his family never stood up for me the only one of them that cared about me was June bug." Darlus would fight me for the least little thing I did or did not know to him for him. He said I was just plain old stupid. I had no concept of what love was or of being in love. I understood submission and obedience; I also understood that every time I did not obey I was beaten. So even if I did not like what was going on I had to submit to whatever would please him.

Darlus took Monique to his sister's house, his girlfriend's house, and his friend's house. He got drunk in his car with her. He never bought her one bag of baby Pampers. When she was old enough to talk he taught her how to call me curse words and other names. I never did bond with my daughter until almost 24 years later. That's how long it took me to understand that her father had caused the rift between me and my daughter. Children only do what you teach them to do. It took me so long to understand that she was only doing what her father taught her to do to me.

My Son Darlus

Eleven months later Darlus would be born. Once again his father was not there. He had put me out of his home in my third month of pregnancy. Friends of his sister 'Flo', Ms. Lena and Ms. Dotty let me stay with them. They took turns, letting me stay in each woman's apartment. Eventually I stayed with Ms. Lena. Darlus put me out this time because he thought the baby was not his. Prior to his having sex with me, he threw me in a room naked to try to make me have sex with his friend, 'Rocky' Max. 'Rocky' never touched me. He put his shirt on me and said, "Let's just sit here and let him think we are doing something so he won't fight with you." And nothing happened; he put his shirt on me and read one of my books to me, because he wanted Darlus to think we were having sex. He went out of the room without his shirt on; then he came back to the room, got his shirt, and left the house. As soon as he left, Darlus came in the room and forced me to have sex with him. The whole time he was asking me if 'Rocky' was happy with my performance. He wanted to know if he did it better than 'Rocky.' How would I know? 'Rocky' never did anything with me. When he finished he beat me because he was talking to me and I did not answer him.

My son Darlus was born at 411 Lafayette Gardens, at a housing project. I felt like something was pushing so I went to the bathroom to take a bath. While sitting in the tub I continued to feel the push, and then I felt what I believe to be a small hand. I began pushing him back inside of me. Darlus' sister 'Flo' came into the bathroom and said, "Gloria, you are having that baby." She helped me onto one of her children's beds and went to call for help. I continued to feel the pushing until I gave birth. Someone handed me a pair of scissors so I could cut his navel cord. They were looking for something to tie his naval cord with. I believe it was 'June Bug' who gave me a clothespin to put on his navel cord. All eight of his cousins and his great uncle 'Bo' watched me give birth to my son. People say they could hear me screaming three blocks away but I could not hear myself. The police came in because someone called them; they thought Darlus was beating me up again. He beat me lots of times while I was pregnant. While I was in the ambulance my son stopped breathing there was supposed to be some kind of machine on the truck but it was not there. I put my hand in his mouth and cleaned it out the best I could. He had started to turn blue. I put my mouth on his mouth and nose and began to suck everything out of his mouth and nostrils and spit it on the floor. My son began to breathe fresh air and cry. The ambulance attendant said "I delivered the baby boy." The doctor said she delivered my son. That was not true. The truth is that I delivered my son by myself with his eight cousins and his great uncle "Bo' standing there watches me. The oldest person there was Uncle 'Bo.' He was 35 years old. I was 19 years old. 'Tiny' was 16 years old, and 'June Bug' was 14 years old. All the rest were young children.

When my son died years later, seven of his eight cousins stood by, and his great uncle 'Bo'; they were the only ones at his burial. All of them were there except for 'June Bug.' His father came to the funeral but he did not stay for the burial; it was only his seven cousins and his Great Uncle 'Bo' who had seen him being born and watched me put him in the ground. People said, "She has gone into shock." But I was not in shock; I was seeing things through the eyes of a child. I could hear them but I could not respond. It was like I was walking through a great maze of people and they all were doing different things, moving about me, but I was not connected to any of them. I was hurt, I was crying once again, but no one could see it or hear me; I was looking from the inside out, through the eyes of a child, too afraid to cry out loud or holler. I just stared back at everything that was around me; no emotions at all did I display, just that blank stare I knew I was there but I felt like I was not. I was somewhere else dancing in my head or being as strong as James Cagney, not cracking a smile and daring anyone to touch me. At the funeral I leaned over to kiss my son for the final time. A lady pulled me up. The look I gave her said it all; she was so terrified she moved to the other side of the church. My son's grandmother did not attend the funeral and neither did my mama. Darlus mother asked the church if she could have the cards that people gave at the wake. My son's grandmother and his father collected all the cards; they took the money from the cards and gave me the empty cards. When one of his cousins, Jerry, saw what my son's father and grandmother were doing with the cards he came directly to me in front of them and put $20 in my hand. Otherwise no one helped me to pay for my son's funeral but Margaret. If it had not been for Margaret taking out insurance on my children and keeping it paid—and up to this day she still pays for their insurance—there would have been no money to bury him with. We had to ask the people at the flower shop if they would trust us until we got back to Georgia, if they would let me have some flowers and we would send the money back to them. We needed the money for his coffin. I said, "We will send you back the money." The man at the flower shop had mercy on me and trusted us, the mercy of Father Yah'uah was there I just did not know it he was in that man at the flower shop. And we sent the money back to him once we got back to Hinesville Georgia. The Spirit of Elohim was in that man's heart; he made sure my son had flowers for his funeral. It's so sad that Father Yah'uah is all around us and we don't see him.

I kept praying in my head the 23rd Psalm over and over again. I was not asking for anything, I was just praying it. The only thing that I really wanted to do was to have sex; I wanted a reason to fight; I wanted to hate; I wanted to be angry; I wanted to destroy something or someone. I took out all of my frustrations and anger on Margaret; I fought her physically and mentally the whole time. She was in my life and she stood by me through all of the madness the homicidal craziness. For me and my children; I'll never understand why she did that. She said something to me while she was driving the car on the freeway; it was nothing harmful or mean. I threw a hot plate of spaghetti in her face and it almost caused a serious accident, but she was still there for my children and me. I was always angry with her most of the time for no reason. I loved her as a person, but I hated her because of what I had to do so my children would not have to be dumb and stupid like me. Margaret could give them the chance to be normal children; she knew what was in books and things about the world around them. She was at that time the only hope I had for my children to be normal and have some quality of life because I had not learned yet about the power of "**Father Yah'uah**" *Elohim* or his son "*Yah'shua*" the Messiah. I only know that God in Jesus Christ existed but I did not know their real names or the power that they were willing to give me to sustain life. I will always respect Margaret for what she did for me in my children.

Darlus was my second child. I loved Darlus from the moment I saw him more than I loved 'Midnight.' He was a handsome baby boy. He was the most beautiful baby boy I had ever seen; he looked exactly like his sister Monique. I was so scared to leave him in the hospital to be circumcised. He never got circumcised. I thought someone would steal my baby boy if I left him in the hospital and I did not want anyone to cut one of my children; I did not want anyone to hurt them. I did not understand the processes or the reason for circumcision. His father did not want him and so that made him my child. But I was afraid of him too, and I was afraid of seeing him naked. So their grandmother Susie Campbell and his cousin Mona Lisa Douglas changed my baby's Pampers and gave him his bath. Mona loved my son. She would sleep in my room so if he cried at night she could change him. I did not want her to feed him I wanted to do that myself. My son was the closest person to me. I never allowed anyone to get as close to my heart as he did. I loved all of my children, but Darlus was the closer to me. When I sent him to school! He would come home from school and be sitting by the door. If he had to leave me he would say, "Mommy, I'm afraid something will happen to you if I'm not here. Did he know that something was very wrong with me? Did he see what I could not see? He said I want to die before you do, because I can't live without you." (He did die before me.) When he was still a baby when I would go to the bars I would take my child with me. When I danced he was on my hip.

Darlus turned four years old when his grandfather saw him for the first time. Darlus was playing with some other children when his grandfather came by. Without anyone telling him which child was his grandson he chose my son. He picked him up and brought him upstairs to us. In the middle of all those children, I asked him, how did he know which child was his grandson? He said Darlus looks like the rest of his family. My son's father is very dark skinned with a red tone. I am brown-skinned but my son's grandfather who is Darlus' father was very light-skinned and so were my father and mother. I thought that is why Darlus came out so light-skinned he never turned dark skin like my daughter so that made his father believe he was not his child but he was Darlus child. He was the jewel of my heart, not because of the color of his skin, but because his father Darlus didn't want him. Darlus' sister 'Flo' and her husband Tom Douglas took care of my son, Darlus, more than any child in the family. Tom took care of Darlus like he was his own son, and they loved him and Monique, but Tom paid special attention to Darlus.

Tutoring by 'June Bug'

'June Bug' helped me name my son. I knew the name that I wanted but I could not spell his name. So Darlus didn't have a name until he was four months old, when 'June Bug' helped me write it on paper. He taught me how to spell all of the names of my children so I could remember how to spell their names, and he taught me how to spell my whole name too. He was always teaching me new things; he taught me how to tell time, and how to count the numbers on the clock. 'June Bug' always helped me to do things that I thought I could not do. He was very patient with me, even though I would constantly make mistakes and get angry and tell myself how stupid I was in that would cause him to say to me you're not stupid do you hear me Gloria. He would say, "You can do it if you stop being so nervous." He never used the word dumb or stupid. He pushed hope down my throat; he made me believe I could do anything if I just kept my mind strong and focused on believing in myself. 'June Bug' also helped me run away from Darlus the first time I left him; I came back because I did not know how to take care of myself in the outside world. I had two children who I was terrified of. I was afraid that I would hurt them like Mama hurt us. I did not know how people took care of themselves or paid bills or how they got jobs. I had always been kept in the house. The only people I associated with were people who let me stay with them. I became their maid, cooking and cleaning their homes and I was their childrens' caregiver. They would let me party with them but I was always kept in the house. 'June Bug' had to explain to me how people got jobs and what they had to do to get them. The first thing he told me was that I would have to go and get on welfare. He said, "You will not stay on welfare long, but right now that is what you need to do; they will send you to school late if you ask them to." But I couldn't even fill out the paperwork. I don't know how he did it, but he got his mother to get the paperwork for me, and she filled it out. All of the check money went for me to get my own place. In the first three months I had saved $400 in a bank account with my name on it. 'June Bug' and his sister, Teresa Douglas—we called her 'Tiny'— they helped me to open up the bank account. The lady at the bank signed my name I was so afraid I forgot the spelling of my name so the lady said to me make an x and that will be your signature but I refuse to so she signed my name for me.

Life in the Welfare Culture

Having my own place was short lived. Darlus knew where I lived. One day he just moved in. I was too afraid of him to say "You cannot stay here." He took the money from my daughter's savings account, and took every check that came in. His niece, 'Tiny,' would come and take me shopping and help me spend whatever food stamps I could hide from Darlus. Otherwise he would sell the stamps and spend the money on all kinds of crazy junk for his car. I had to think of ways to keep Pampers and baby food for my babies. He never spent one dime on Pampers or on his children. He loved saying "I'm the father", but he had no clue what a father was or did.

Even today men love to say "I'm the father" and do nothing for their children. I had a father, but he wasn't a father who lived in the home. He came once a year and brought clothing, toys, coloring books and crayons, paper and pencils, and shoes for us. Once a year he got to play father the sad part is `that the children who are like me always really love their parents. Some of you mothers know what I'm talking about. There were weekend fathers who came on the weekend to spend the night with the mothers. Then there were fathers who were with the children from Monday through Thursday. On Friday they were gone with their paychecks. Then there were lazy fathers who wouldn't work in a pie factory, even if they got all the pies they wanted for free. Then there were those bum fathers. All they did was eat up all the food in the house, then go to another girlfriend's house. When everything was gone at her house, he would come back to yours house to see what you had scrounged up for your kids and then he word eat that and complain that all you care about is the kids. Then there were those fathers who came by once a month to see their kids, not to give them anything but just so he could say he came by. What he was really doing was making sure you didn't have another man helping you. He didn't give you anything, but he did not want another man to help you and he didn't want to see you with anything or you getting ahead. And there were those 'check day fathers' who only came on the first and the 15th of each month. That was the only time their children saw them. They came to collect the checks from the Department of Social Services from the mothers on the first and the 15th. They were no real fathers. We used to call them 'check day daddies.' They would say, "Hey 'Baby,' can you give me a couple of them food stamps too? You know I love you, 'Baby.' Hey there, 'Baby,' got any more of that welfare cheese? How about butter? I need some 'because my mother wants to bake me a cake." I used to think, "Why your mother won't bake a cake for her grandchildren?" Oh, I almost forgot one, father we call him 'I am not going to work anywhere father' who refused to keep a job. When he got a job he would go in late, miss some days, or leave the job early and come home. Then he would blame the boss when he lost the job. He would say, "Those white men's want to keep us black men down. "Those were all the fathers I knew. We women made sure the checks and the food stamps were coming for our children, but these so-called fathers made sure our children did not benefit from the money, and then they would complain that the white man was always keeping them down. Had they really looked in the mirror they would've seen it was they themselves keeping their family down, not the white man? They did not allow themselves to be responsible for their own children or wives or live-in women—today we call them 'significant others.' The man made it his own choice to go for the money rather than to help his children and wife or the woman he was living with at the time to do better It was another work of Satan, not the work of the white man. And certainly not the work of Father Yah'uah. It was Satan in camp in these fathers to make sure another generation of his children would not succeed in life history repeating itself.

Exemplary Men

I praise "**Father Yah'uah**" *Elohim* for the real fathers and men that I have met since I have become a Christian. I've seen black men like James Hill or Roy Tunnage loving and nurturing their families, leading them in the direction of honesty, wholeness, and happiness, not discouraging or distrusting or controlling or dominating them, but loving them like a father should. These fathers were leading their wives and their children in all the things that I did not have or did not see other children have as I grew up. Mr. Roy Tunnage respected his wife and his children as himself. He lovingly and cared for his family with all the respect of a father so they would know the love of their Heavenly Father, "**Yah'uah**" Elohim, and that they were special individuals yet also part of a whole family. He demanded that they treat people with the utmost respect even if others weren't being pleasant to them. I respected him the most for that more than anything else, because I was seeing for the first time a black father (who was not on television) taking care of his own wife and children without getting them to manipulate the system. He was the breadwinner, the family protector and the problem solver for his family and when he was not at home his wife Ms. Debbie acted like he was still there carrying out the function of the family.

Exemplary Women

I had seen a lot of strong black mothers who was raising children so streetwise but they knew nothing about the Bible only right and wrong in how to run the game. But Ms. Deborah who is Ms. Debbie was the first black mother that I ever seen who was a strong but gentle black mother. Ms. Deborah Tunnage never once belittled her children or took sides with them when they were wrong. She honestly loved her children as a mother should. They were not for sale at any price. She taught them how to do things the right way. She explained things to them. She had a good relationship with her children. She gave them room to make mistakes yet she showed them how to correct the mistakes they made. She didn't just tell them about God **"Father Yah'uah"** *Elohim*, she helped them to understand how to live for Him. She taught them that every man and woman is a servant for each other's and that they should love the unlovable just as *"Yah'shua"* the Messiah loves them. She did not just put on a show for people; it was the way she really lived for the love of *"Yah'shua"* the Messiah. Ms. Deborah made the Bible come alive for her children every story she interact with them with lots of questions and very good answers I was learning again in silence. She made sure her children understood every story that they read together from the Bible. She didn't just talk the Bible to them, she lived the Bible with them, and she helped them to love others I remember once this lady had my checkbooks she said she was having my tax done for me in reality her and her lawyer was trying to use my books to pretend she had donated to the heart of Christ Inc. And Yah Gives a Second Chance Ministry the two organizations. When I figured it out I asked her for the books back she got aggressive with me I was going to beat her like a Hebrew slave but Mr. and Mrs. Tonnage decided to take me to get the books I did not want to do anything bad in front of Ms. Deborah I was going to wait until the lady got close enough to the van and I was going to kick her in her face and take my box I had seen so many times how on television how to beat somebody senseless and throw them out of the van was Father Yah'uah there he was in Mr. Roy and Ms. Deborah saving that lady or me from a beat down. Ms. Debbie always loved her children even when she was correction them. She was that way with people to in a gentle way so I did not bet that lady up that day. Ms. Debbie taught her children how to be calm-mannered and show them how to give respect to other adults and children secretly I was learning from her and Mr. Roy. She also taught her children that they are somebody very special. She is all the things that a mother is supposed to be. She and her husband have faults as we all do, but their commitment to each other and to their children it is there real lifestyle. It was not an act that they put on for people; it was their lifestyle that they honored Father Yah'uah with. **"Father Yah'uah"** *Elohim* blessed me to know them. I keep a picture of the whole family in a room separate from all the rest of the pictures I have; it is a reminder to me what a family is and what a family is supposed to be.

Life With Darlus

At my house I was kept in a room in the house with my two children all the time. The only time I came out was to cook and clean. My only visitors were 'June Bug' and 'Tiny.' Everybody else came because of Darlus. He would bring his girlfriends to my house, and I had to cook and clean for them. My youngest sister 'Koochie Mama' would come, too. I knew she was coming to be with Darlus, but I didn't care; it gave me more time with my children. She would help me with changing their Pampers and giving them baths. I really never had the children for long periods of time; by myself 'Flo' would always get them from me. Darlus would bring men to the house and fight with me to force me to have sex with them. I never saw money change hands, but I believe it did. One day while cleaning he said to me, "I really love you and you're never going to leave me because I won't let you. I own you, girl." I had stopped trying to run away because now I had two children to worry about. But I wanted so much for them to have a better chance than I did. So I began to hide money that I would steal from my check so that I could run way from Darlus.

George Lesroy Wynter

I met my husband George Lesroy Wynter when Darlus brought him to the house. We called him 'Winnie.' I was in the room with my two babies, Monique and Darlus, when they came in. Darlus called me from the room to fix them food and give them ice and glasses so they could begin their night of drinking. I would have to return to my room. Until about three in the morning when they were finish drinking 'Winnie' knocked on the door. When I answered he said, "Come and lock the front door." He left the next night. When he came again he said he was meeting 'Koochie Mama,' so the three of them drank whiskey into the wee hours of the morning. The name of the whiskey that Darlus liked was 'Fighting Cock.' It was 130 proof. My sister and Darlus had passed out. Once again 'Winnie' knocked on the door. I said, "What do you want now?" He said, "For you to help me put your man to bed." I opened the door and came out of the room. He helped me drag Darlus into the bedroom and then lift him onto the bed. I said, "You have to go now." He said, "Let's put your sister to bed." So we put her in the children's room so she could sleep it off. 'Winnie' helped me clean up the living room and the kitchens, wash the dishes and glasses, and put them away. I said, "You have to go now, 'Winnie'." He said, "Why?" I replied, "If Darlus wakes up he will fight you." He said, "I can take care of myself. But I want to know, why do you stay with him?" I paused for a few minutes to think about what this guy was doing, asking me that question. Then I said. "I have no place else to go." He said, "Come with me." I thought, "I don't even know you." He said, "You're beautiful, what are you doing with him?" I said, "Please leave before I get in trouble." And he left. I had only had one other person tell me that I was beautiful I had never had a man say those words to me that I was beautiful. 'June Bug' had said I was beautiful, but I thought he just felt sorry for me. I thought he knew I was ugly, but he did not want to make me feel bad about myself. That's why he said I was beautiful. 'June Bug' never wanted me to feel bad about anything. So I really didn't believe him.

Every single night for about two weeks 'Winnie' would come with a bottle of 'Fighting Cock' and a big box of Kentucky fried chicken. 'Koochie Mama' would come too, and every night we would put them to bed. One particular night my sister and Darlus had gone into the children's room and gone to bed. After 'Winnie' knocked on the door he took me straight to the room where they were in bed necked asleep in each other's arms. I showed no emotion, I wasn't upset, I just looked in, turned around and left the room. He said, "Don't you care?" And I replied, "No, I don't." As we cleaned up the living room and kitchen, he talked to me. He said, "Do you want to get away from him?" I said, "Yes, but I have nowhere to go." He said, "You could stay with me." I did not know if he was just feeling sorry for me, because I thought he really liked my baby sister 'Koochie Mama.' When I walked him to the door he said, "Look up at me," because I always kept my head down. I was concerned about Darlus waking up and seeing me talking to someone that he had not given me permission to. When I looked up he kissed me. The kiss did not mean anything to me. I just was shocked that he did it. He said to me, "Get some things packed, we're leaving. I will be back for you tomorrow night."

The next day I was rushing around trying to find things for my babies and myself. I was so nervous that whole day until that night, but 'Winnie' did not show up. A whole week went by and no 'Winnie.' Then out of the blue after Darlus got home, 'Winnie' knocked on the door. He said, "Hi, man. I have a little something, something for you man." He had a half gallon of 'Fighting Cock' and a bag of reefers. Darlus did not drink as much as usual. He came into the bedroom and said, "Go out there with him." I said, "There is nobody to take care of the children." He said, "Get out there now." So I came out of the room. I kept my head down, not saying a word to Winnie. 'Winnie' got up and left the house. The next night he and 'Koochie Mama' came. Darlus had told me that morning he wanted me to fry some chicken and fish and make French fries. He said they were having a party, and I was to stay in the room. I had to put all the baby bottles in the room because he didn't want me out of the room. I said, "I will fry the fish and chicken but I do not want to peel and fry potatoes." He said, "Gloria, just fry the potatoes." He gave me the money to buy beer and the whiskey from the store. As usual I did what I was told. They party all night. 'Winnie' did not drink. He said Darlus was watching him all that night. After Darlus passed out, 'Winnie' knocked on the door to tell me to get my clothing. Darlus got up asking, "Where is everybody? Why are you still in my house? And what are you doing out of the room?" My heart stopped because I knew the fight was about to start when Darlus grabbed hold of me and started punching me. 'Winnie' started fighting him. I ran out of the house downstairs and into the neighbor's apartment. Everybody was watching the fight. The neighbors did not know that I was hiding in their apartment. Darlus and 'Winnie' fought all the way downstairs and out of the building into the middle of the street. Someone call the police when they came everybody started hurrying back into their apartment and into their houses. When the neighbors came back to their apartment, they saw me. I had seen them lots of times but had never talked to them. They wanted me out of their house. The lady was saying, "I don't want him to come and fight us." She was right, he would have if he knew I was in there, her husband went upstairs to see what Darlus was doing. He came back downstairs and said, "He's sleeping." They pushed me out of the front door of their apartment. As soon as I stepped outside 'Winnie' came out from behind a building. He said, "Let's go." I said, "I can't." He said, "Why not, you're out of the house now!" I said, "I can't leave my children and I'm afraid to go up and get them." He said, "Stay here." He went upstairs and got my two children. We had to take a cab to another part of Brooklyn that I had never been to or seen. A lot of 'Jewish' people lived in that area.

'Winnie' was a painter and a hotel manager. He put me and the babies in a room that night. He and my babies slept in the bed, and I slept in the chair the next morning when I woke up he and my children were gone. I panicked because I did not know where he had gone with them. When he came back he had breakfast for us. We sat on the floor with a blanket and ate breakfast. Then he asked me if I would live with him. I was thinking, was he out of his mind? I just got away from Darlus but I didn't have a job or money to take care of my babies and myself. The money I had saved was still at the house and I was not going back! For it, it was not like I loved or felt anything for 'Winnie,' but I said, "If you really want me you'll have to marry me." He balled his mouth up and thought about it and said, "Why?" I said, "Because I want a father for my children." He asked me then if I loved him. I replied that I didn't, but I would stay faithful to him and I did.

We got married in October on his birthday. The day we got married his brother and my sister, 'Koochie Mama,' was there. Right after the marriage I had to clean every empty room in the hotel, mop the floors and take out the garbage cans. That was my honeymoon. The second night my husband wanted to have sex with me, but he had me working from sunup till sundown, plus cooking and taking care of my children. 'Koochie Mama' helped me give my children baths. She was a big help to me in lots of ways. We helped each other. We had always done that; all of us children would take care of each other. The next day 'Winnie' had 'Koochie Mama' takes my babies to a playground and have, lunch out there he gave her a couple of dollars. He forced himself on me. He forced me until I just gave in. He said, "You have to pay your way here." That is what married life was like for me.

I'd remember the 23rd Psalm every time he would beat me or sleep with other women in the hotel or with 'Koochie Mama.' I would ask 'God, Father Yah'uah' for my children's sake to help me become a good mother. I started planning from that day how to get away from 'Winnie.' Eventually he started working in a bar. We call those types of bars 'holes in the wall.' After real bars closed, people would come and party until daybreak. This bar was below street level; you opened two iron doors in order to go down into the rooms from the street. It was a cellar or basement; people used them for storage rooms. My husband built a bar and he and the owner of the building used the cellar for an after hours nightclub. He would bring white women into our home. He would send me downstairs to work in the bar while he spent time with them. We had two beds in the house; his brother and my sister shared one and I and my children and husband shared the other. He would put my children on the floor when he would sleep with white women in the bed. If I said anything, he would beat me. His brother did not like the way 'Winnie' treated me. He would save me a lot of times. His brother was a very good man. Eventually he moved out of the apartment. He never once spoke evil to me about his brother although he did not like the way he treated me.

I called Darlus' mother and asked her if she would rent me a room in her apartment. She agreed and I went to live in her house again. 'Winnie' and Darlus would have fights all the time. 'Winnie' would steal me off of the street if I went to the store. He would get a car and someone to drive for him, and then he would throw me in the backseat and hold me down. He tied me up in the apartment. He would board up the doors and lock all of the windows and nailed them shut. It was more about whose property I was and who would have ownership of me. I was not a person to them. I was property. I promised my children I would get them out of this mess no matter what I had to do. I wanted "**Father Yah'uah**" *Elohim* to help me but I did not know how to live 'godly.' All I did know was the 23rd Psalm. I could not stand to say the name of 'Jesus Christ' because of the preacher who used to come to Mama's house, and how he used the name of 'Jesus' while he was rape me. One day I just got my kids and went back to Darlus' mother's apartment. I was going in circles because I had nowhere to go, and this cycle kept repeating itself. I still had not asked 'Jesus' ("*Yah'shua*") for his help.

My Son Lesroy

I found out after I left 'Winnie' that I was two months pregnant with my third child and my second son, Lesroy. My son was born in front of a jailhouse. I was going to visit someone when I went in labor. I can't feel pain the way other people do, so I gave birth to my son on the street. I was taken to Long Island College Hospital after he was born. When I first looked at him I started crying. I said to the nurse, "That is not my baby." She said, "Why are you saying that?" I said, "Because he's gray and a lot of skin is hanging off of him." She said to me, "This will be the most beautiful child you have." And she was right; my son is a handsome young man. Giving birth gave me a little breathing room from Darlus. Susie helped me with my son like she did with all the other children. Mona, her granddaughter, took care of him the most. They knew I could not handle seeing my children naked. They did not know why I couldn't stand to see my children naked

Was the Spirit of "**Father Yah'uah**" there in all of that mess? He was. I just couldn't recognize Him or hear His call. I kept looking to people to be my source and provider and wallowing in the same filthy lifestyle I wanted to get away from but I didn't know how to get out of it. I would ask 'God' in the name of 'Jesus' to help me; then I would do whatever I wanted to do. But "**Father Yah'uah**" is patient with His children, guiding them ever so gently so they can come to Him through His Son, "*Yah'shua*" the Messiah.

Escaping From Darlus

I ran away from Darlus again. This time I did not let anyone know where I was except for my caseworker. Somehow Darlus found out where I was so I had to go back home. All of the checks that the welfare gave me went straight to him and his mother. I started going to school so I could learn to read, but Darlus fussed and argued and tore up my books and threw my clothes away. Sometimes he beat me so badly I couldn't walk. I was too afraid to fight him back. I needed a place for my children to live so I stayed with him and tolerated the beatings.

One day my oldest son Darlus was playing on the floor with a handkerchief. He threw it up in the air and it came down in his father's plate of food. Darlus slapped him so hard his nose started bleeding. I had never fought Darlus back. When I heard my son screaming and I saw his father standing over him, I begged him, saying "Please doesn't hurt him, please don't hit him." He was saying the child was not his. I kept walking toward the kitchen talking to big Darlus , trying to keep my child from fussing so he would not be hurt. Darlus called my son every curse word he could possibly think of but as long as he wasn't hitting him, I could handle the rest. He went back to the living room and I came to get the baby who started crying as soon as he saw his father. Then Darlus went after my son again I ran to the kitchen and grabbed a knife. He had hit him and then said, "Shut up right now." I couldn't think. All I knew at that moment was that I was not going to let him hurt my child. Darlus sat back in the chair and started eating as I was coming up the hall. When I got into the living room he was still fussing and eating. All I had on was my bra and panties. I took that knife and stabbed him in the leg and through the back of his hand; I pinned his hand to the chair. I grabbed my baby and ran down those four flights of steps straight to the police station. My daughter and my baby were still in the apartment with their grandmother. The police station was on the next corner. There were people chasing me because they thought something was wrong with the baby. When I got inside my son had handprints all over the back part of his back and legs. What I didn't know was that Darlus was running behind me too. When he got inside the police station he ran over to the officer who was talking to me and he knocked me down with the baby in my arms. Those police officers in that police station, I mean everybody that had a blue suit on, and detectives began beating him. I was helping them to. They lock him up. His mother said if I pressed charges, they would take my children from me. I was afraid to tell the judge what happened. His mother bailed him out of jail.

Darlus allowed me to go back to school for awhile, as long as I gave him the welfare checks. I got money for going to school. I got money for daycare. I got money for rent and money to travel, about $150 for travel expenses every two weeks. That's what took care of my babies' Pampers and food. The other checks they kept. I would walk to school but so much was going on in my head I could not learn anything. I was always thinking about how to get away. It was 'June Bug' who kept encouraging me to leave. He said, "Just save up some money and you will be able to go." He would give me any extra money he got for doing odd jobs for people. We were young teenagers. There was nothing sexual about our relationship. He was just good to me and really treated me as though I was his best aunt. "In the world," he said, "every star has a name and 'God' has named a star after you."

I left Darlus' shortly after that because I just couldn't take it anymore. I did not have a place to stay. So my children and I slept that night at the subway station. The next day I got a shopping cart, put my babies in it and went shopping. I bought piles of food, all kinds of junk food: lunchmeat, bread, milk, fruit, and bags of ice. And then I went looking for an abandoned house for us to stay in, and I found one. We lived in that abandoned house for a long time. It was in a white neighborhood. Someone called the police on me. They told me I had to leave.

I went to 'Hot Mama' and I left my babies there. I told Darlus I would come back if he did not take my children from me. He said "Okay," but they had already reported me to child protective services. That very day I had found an apartment for me and my babies. Darlus and his mother had me summoned into court. The lady at the courthouse said they just wanted to see the children to make sure they were all right. I had to bring them in so the judge could see them. The next day I took my kids into court with me. The lady came and said to me, "We have a playroom for children and we will feed them lunch. You can come and look at the room and see how many children are in there. Your children will be comfortable and happy." When I saw all of the children laughing and playing I said "okay" and I let her take my children and put them in that room. When I got inside the courtroom Darlus and his mother came through another door. They accused me of letting my daughter fall down a flight of steps. I was in school when that happened, and she was in the care of her grandmother. They also accused me of not taking care of my kids, not giving them baths. I didn't give them baths but the grandmother and Mona big sister of 'June Bug' in my baby sister did. The judge asked me to give my two older children to their father and grandmother. I said, "No." He said they would have to keep them until I got a job and found a place to live. I told the judge I had never had a real job that Darlus had paid my mama $500 for me when I was 12 years old and every time I tried to go to school he fought me. The judge said, "Since you have been with this man all of this time then he is your first husband, and he has the same rights as you do. If you get a job, I'll give you back your kids." Then he said, "This is the last time I'm going to ask you this. Do you want the father and grandmother to raise them?" I said, "No. I will get a job and find a place."

Interactions With Social Workers

He assigned a social worker to me. She would take me to see my kids. Every time I had to go back to court so the judge could see how I was doing, she would have a new complaint against me. Once my daughter stomped her brother's leg and I said to her, "Monique that was not nice. Would you like Mommy to jump and stomp your leg?" She said, "No Mommy." When I went to court the social worker said I threatened to stomp my child's leg. While I was working I bought all the clothes for my children but whenever I saw them they had rags on close that were too small for them or raggedy. I had given the clothes to the social worker, I complained to her about the way my children looked not to the foster mother. She told the judge that I make the foster mother nervous. That was a lie. The social worker thought I was a bigoted person. I was not. I was just standing up for my children. No one had ever stood up for us so I was not going to let anyone take advantage of my children, under no circumstances! All the social worker did was brought more sorrow in my life. She did not want me to get my children back. My son got hit in the head with a swing. He wasn't taken to the hospital and he got some type of infection. When I saw him I demanded he be taken to the hospital. I went to see him in the hospital. He said, "Mommy, why don't you love us anymore?" I don't know why I walked out of the room. I could hear myself screaming. I was screaming at the top of my voice. I passed out in that hallway. They said I was unstable. They put me in a mental institution. I was emotionally and physically and mentally drained. I had no one to fight for me or for my children. I had had to fight my entire life. So now my son who had to be about three or four years old believe I did not love them or care what happens to them. My children had to stay in foster care for a year and a half because the court ordered me to see a psychologist. I don't remember anything about my visits to the psychologist but he recommended my children be given back to me.

I got my own place. I moved to Brooklyn, NY into a big apartment building. I lived on the fourth floor. It had two bedrooms, a bathroom, a large kitchen and living room. It was just enough for me and my babies. I stopped going to school because I did not want Darlus to try to take my children from me. But I did not do very well with my children. I mean, I loved them but if you've been hit all your life, you have the tendency to hit. I did not allow anyone, I mean no one, to hit one of my children but I would hit them and then get depressed because I had. So most of the time, I paid other people to look after them so they could be safe from me I would go out at night and party at nightclubs *as long as I was dancing. I was in a fantasy world of my own dancing always takes me into another place.*

More on Visions and Voices

As I began to get older I knew I was different than everybody else. Sometimes it frightened me because of the different things I saw or heard. I have been like this for my entire life. As I have said, I did not know that people did not see things or hear voices. The voices sound like someone talking to me from a distance or like someone whispering in my ear. Sometimes I was seeing things through the eyes of a child. The visions would show me exactly what I was supposed to do although I did not have prior knowledge.

For instance, one time a friend of my husband 'Winnie' named Johnson he lived at my apartment with me, but he had his own apartment, but it was closer to go to school from my apartment. He was going to school to fix radios. He needed to build a radio from different parts that they had provided for him. He could not put the radio together. He was so afraid he would fail the tests. One night after he had worked on it for hours and hours, he went to bed. I got the box and looked at the box for awhile. Everything I needed to do I could see so clearly in my head. I could hear and see where to put every wire; every piece had its shape and place. The colors on the box itself helped me. My mind's eye could see exactly what to do. By morning I had put the whole radio together. When I turned it on it played good and loud, but I could not explain to Johnson how I had done it.

Another time I was in this program that the state had provided for me to attend, and they wanted to know our level of understanding so they gave us different things to do. One of the things was to make a belt. They gave us buckles and leather pieces that had to be looped together. "That is so easy," I thought; "anybody could do that." Then they gave us different puzzles to put together; that were easy too.

One of the janitors was trying to put a stepladder together. He was having so much trouble doing it, so when they sat down to have lunch I picked up the paper, looked at the diagram, and began putting the ladder together. The picture on the paper helped me the most. It was not a big deal to me. I heard the voice in my head tell me what to do. It went something like this: "Put that down; that doesn't go there; pick up the other piece; yes, that goes there; you just have one more piece now." When I finished putting the ladder completely together everybody's mouths were open and they were staring at me. They took the ladder apart again and asked me to put it together for them again, and I did it. I did not know why they asked me that; I think they did not think I was able to put the ladder together without being able to read the instructions every step of the way. The Bible says "For the gifts and the calling of God are irrevocable" (Romans 11:29, NKJV).

I've heard voices tell me what to do lots of times. I will not tell anyone I hear voice inside of my head because I do not want anyone to be afraid of me or think that I am crazy. Sometimes the hardest thing for me is controlling the voice. I will know something that needs to be done and I will not do it even though I could hear the exact way to do it. People always seem to question me and think either I already knew how to do it or they think I was just pretending or lying. Sometimes I just wait until they walk away, then I will do what needs to be done. I cannot allow them to know what I see and hear; that part of me I keep hidden from people, because they will not be able to understand me because I cannot give them an explanation why this happens to me. They think I do not comprehend what they're telling me, but I do. If a word is too big I will ask them to explain it to me. It is the way I'd come up with the right answer that makes them frightened, so I do not tell them anything at all.

About Margaret

My heart was always good to people. If you did not try to dominate me or make me do something that I said "no" to, we had no problems; but if you tried to force me to do anything it was trouble for you or anyone who tried. I had one thing in mind: I had to protect my children and myself at all costs. There was this person I would see come in and out of the building. He had on a hat that covered most of his face, a long black coat, blue jeans, and a boy's shirt. He would always ask me for a dollar. I thought it was a teenager or a young man. I felt sorry for him. One day he was drunk sleeping in the hallway. That night he was still sleeping in the hallway.

My children and I dragged him into my apartment. He smelled terrible. So I cut the clothes off of him and I saw that 'he' was a 'she!' After I got the clothes off of her, I washed her and put a pillow under her head and covered her up. I put clean clothes in the bathroom and some underwear, toothpaste and toothbrush, comb and brush, clean socks, pants and blouse, washcloth, a bath towel and soap, and a bottle of perfume. When I woke up she had prepared breakfast for my children, and she was sitting in the room reading a book to my daughter. She didn't say a word to me and I didn't talk to her. She asked me a little later on in the day if she could have a dollar. I gave her five dollars. I had had a man friend but had gotten rid of him some time ago, so it was just me and my children.

They took to Margaret well. She was very patient with my children. Lesroy was almost 2 years old and she had already taught him how to read some words. Monique and Darlus were reading as well. I used to stand by the door and listen to her read to them. She would make the story come alive for them. She would be telling them things and they would be answering questions. She played games with them every day; she put on talent shows with them every week. Margaret was real good to my children. She did not have children of her own, so my children became her children and Margaret loved them and they loved her. Until this day she still has a relationship with them.

She asked me one day why I was so distant from people. I said to her, "You're not a people person either." From that day on we began to talk about everything. She wanted to be with me. I wanted her in my life for my children's sake. They would have a chance to learn how to read and write, how to count, and most of the time she saved them from being hit by me. Whenever I wanted to hit them, she and I would end up fighting each other. She would always lose the fight, but she would fight me back. I would throw hot water on her, bite her, and hit her with anything I got my hand on. I would stab and cut her with knives at those times I would lose total control, but I knew she was the best person to help raise my children. Whenever she would be with me sexually, I would really get sick. I would throw up and then stay in the shower for long periods of time, just crying some time she would ask what was wrong. I did not know what was wrong I would just get that way; I would scrub myself with bleach. I would leave my home for days, but I knew I could not get rid of her. She was at that time the only hope I had for my children not being dumb or stupid like me, so I made the choice to live an 'ungodly' life. Margaret took a lot of stuff from me, but she stayed for my children. She would not let me hurt them, even though she knew if she interfered when I was chastising them there would be a fight between her and me, but she protected my children with a vengeance. I put Margaret through many terrifying situations for no reasons.

Margaret joined the Army and then went overseas. She wrote my children letters, sent them boxes home, and made sure they had money for their allowances and money in the bank. My children did not lack for anything. The biggest problem they had was me. I had learned a lot from Margaret. I had a choice to make. I chose to stay with her, even though I was totally out of control when she had sex with me. My life was okay with her as long as we did not have sex. I stayed away from home most of the time. She wanted to know why I acted the way I did to her. She did know some of the things that had happened to me, but I could never bring myself to remember everything that had happened to me. Whenever I wanted to go out she would try to fight me to make me stay home. I was afraid of hurting my children, and I was afraid of killing her. I knew I needed her, but I was angry every time she had sex with me, but for my children's sake I knew I had to keep her. I could not give them the things she could. She could give them the teaching and learning that I could not so I chose hell rather than life. I asked her one day why she stayed with me as long as she did. She said, "The way I see you take care of people is so pure and innocent. I don't know why you treat me so badly, Gloria."

I put Margaret through so many terrifying situations for no reasons. I always started a fight with her. I cannot remember one time she started a fight with me. She would say something and I would start a fight. The last time I did something awful to Margaret was when I cut her stomach open. I cannot tell you to this day why I did that to her. I really don't remember. She was sitting by the front door holding everything that came out of her stomach in her hands. I called the police. She would not tell the police I had cut her like that. After I did it, I had thrown the big butcher knife on the bed. Although there were no sheets or blankets on the bed, the police could not see the butcher knife. They asked me what happened. I could not tell them. I had stopped talking and Margaret would not tell on me. I was seeing things through the eyes of a child. When the police asked her, she said she had fallen down on the butcher knife. They knew she was lying. She had to be flown from Hinesville Hospital to Savannah Hospital. She stayed in the hospital about a month. It was the last bad thing I did to Margaret. I left the house with no where to go, and I lived on the street. I was afraid I was going to kill her. I never lived in the house with her again after that. Every day I pray and told **"Father Yah'uah"** how sorry I am for the bad choices I made in my life and for hurting Margaret so badly she did not deserve my anger and rage. I pray that Margaret would forgive me and that

"Father Yah'uah" would forgive me through "*Yah'shua*" my Messiah.

I could tell you a lot of bad things Margaret did to me. But I won't, because the best thing she did for me is to bring up my children to be decent and loving people. My son, Lesroy, does not hit his children. He and his wife have patience with them and have an abundance of love for my grandchildren. And I will always be grateful to Margaret for that. She saved my children from their worst nightmare that they could have had; that nightmare was me. After my children became young teenagers my youngest son was 17 years old I started going to church every chance I got; I knew I could not handle the life that Satan had planned out for me. "*Yah'shua*" the Messiah had to have something better for me than I had for myself. I did not care what it was; all I knew was I had to have it.

Darlus' Fate

My son Darlus was killed for his coat. I had seen his death before he was born. The night of his death, I pulled every dish out of the cabinet and broke them on the floor. I told Margaret, "Darlus is dead." She said, "Gloria, it's not true. Let's call him." When I talked to him, I had asked him not to go out of the house. He said, "Okay Mommy." I asked my sister Hot Mama not to let my child out of her house. She said, "Okay, 'Peewee.'" He had asked me not to go out that night. He said, "Mommy, when are you going to stop partying?" My children never knew my lifestyle or what went on in my Mama's house; all they knew was that I would stay away from home a lot. They had no real clue why I did or how I was brought up. I never told them anything about my Mama. They just knew they couldn't stay there at her home. I believe they saw her maybe four times in their lives. I did not want them around her. I did not want her to hurt my children at all, not even with harsh words.

Monique and Lesroy

My children are very close to one another. Lesroy looks after Monique and me a lot. Monique works, but her brother will save up money and send it to her, or save up money to send to me. I try not to ask him for anything, but when he knows I'm in need he does the best he can and that's such a good thing. My son has four children of his own. He does not abuse his wife or children, he never allows them to fight one another, and they have never known a hungry day. I would never allow my children to fight one another. Once I let Lesroy give his big sister a good old-fashioned beating. She knew she wasn't supposed to fight him, but she kept hitting him every time she got around her father's family members. He kept telling me she was doing it and I kept talking to her. She continued that behavior. I told Lesroy if she hit him again he could go ahead and fight her back, and that is exactly what he did. I just couldn't stay in the house to see them fight one another. He never had any more trouble out of her after that. My children do not tell me if someone did something to them, not even today, because they know that I would do something hideous to that person. If an adult did something to one of my children, there is no place that adult could go to hide from me. I would not even allow any teachers to put their hands on my children. If they hit my children, not only me would they have to fight, but also everyone that knew me.

Generosity and Defensiveness

I came to Georgia because I had done so many bad things in New York. A police officer friend of mine said, "You have to leave for awhile, Gloria." I had started selling drugs, so I had bodyguards, Carlos and Ricky, are Spanish young men. They took care of me whenever I was in the street selling drugs. When I made money I would use that money to help people. I would buy them food and clothing, and pay their rent. I'd pay doctor bills, light bills, gas bills, and water bills, make sure their kids had clothes to go to school, and their kids could stay in college. But I also was a tyrant. I was mean as anything once when I was in the nightclub. A woman spilled drinks on me and burned me with her cigarettes every time I walked by if I was on the dance floor. She would burn or spill her drank on me. I had had enough. I felt like she was breathing too much of my air and I could not breathe. So I started a fight and I beat her up. I did not talk a lot. If I was talking to you, you'd know I wanted to work things out with you. It is when I got quiet that you knew there was a problem, because while I'm quiet I'm seeing things through the eyes of a child. I am not just acting. I am thinking in my head, "I have got to stop you from hurting me."

"*Yah'shua*" the Messiah has brought me a long way. Later when I had become a Christian I could not protect myself anymore; I had to learn how to let **"Father Yah'uah"** and Yahshua the Messiah, and the Holy Spirit do that for me. And that was hard for me to do in the beginning. I had lived in my own world; now I had to live in the normal world and sometimes the real world was just as frightening as Mama's house was.

Relationships with Women and Men

I seemed to intimidate most women. I was built with a pear-shaped body. I have a large bottom and a small waistline. I could not help the way I was built, but it has caused a lot of problems for me. I think I gained weight on purpose, but I didn't realize it until I began writing this book. I wanted to have friends and not have women feel afraid of me or think I was after their husbands. I am probably the one person a woman could trust around her husband. I did not want any of my own husbands; I certainly did not want their husbands or their problem—I had enough of my own! I did not have a man in my life. For 24 years I had had a male friend as my best friend. One of my friends said, "I would not want my husband to be friends with you." For 23 or 24 years until that day I did not know it was wrong to have another woman's husband as my best friend. She asked, "What would other women think?" So she said "I would not want my husband to be friends with you." I broke off our friendship. I started a fight with him about everything. He had never approached me in any sexual manner; he was just my friend. Michael was a very good Christian man and a wonderful friend.

I had another friend. I had given her and about four of her girlfriends and her sister massages. She came and asked me to give her brother-in-law one. I said to his wife, "Stay in the room with me" so she could see nothing inappropriate went on; nothing happened inappropriately. The wife came in the room and then she left. I thought everything was okay in that she trusted me, nothing else. The same woman who asked to give her brother-in-law a massage she came to my shop and asked me to give her son a massage. I said, "He's 18 years old." I didn't want to, but she said everybody had talked about how good the massage was and she paid me eighty dollars. I had never been paid to give someone a massage. So I agreed to do it if she would stay in the room. After I finished giving him the massage she was very upset. She said, "What was that all about?" I had done the same thing to him as I had done to her and everyone else. I had never had anyone teach me how to give someone a massage or anyone treat me bad because of a massage. We had to do them for people that came to Mama's house; that's how I'd known how to give them. This woman likes to control everything in everybody in her life. When she couldn't control me with money she found a weapon to use against me. She was wealthy and had a very bad habit of controlling everything with her money. Why would I ask the mother to sit there to make sure nothing inappropriate went on? I cried so much over that incident. It really broke my heart. I have never given another person a massage since that day, no matter what they offered to pay me.

I had a friend, a very good friend. I could actually talk to her about anything, and she helped me with so many things. She helped me with my shop. She helped me with my clients. When a homeless dog I was taking care of died, she and her husband came and helped a young man bury him for me. I trusted her and respected her so much; that was about to change. I have not allowed myself to trust anyone for a very long time or get very close to me.

Curt and Gretchen Wagner

At the beginning of this book I said my father and mother are Dr. Curt Wagner and his wife, Gretchen. In my heart he is my true father and his wife, my true mother. **"Father Yah'uah"** *Elohim* had put it in their hearts to provide a place where I could carry on my spiritual ministry people could come and stay they did not have a home for at least 30 days at a time and I could continue to renew the lease. If they needed more time, Also Christians who were on drugs had a place where they could come to whether it out. It also is use for the poor of the area. It is an extension of the heart of Christ, incorporation I had already established a 501c3 ministry for '**YAH** Gives A Second Chance Ministry.' When the opportunity arose to buy a 2 acre piece of **land** in rural Glennville, I told the Wagners I was praying for land and they immediately knew it was the will of **"Father Yah'uah"** to buy the property for the Ministry! The next step was to acquire some kind of a building from which I could minister. I knew what **"Father Yah'uah"** had shown me in a vision, so we started looking for some kind of a mobile home trailer. Eventually we found a triple-wide mobile home that would match my vision and also was at a reasonably priced. It had a very large family-type room that would work perfectly as a 'sanctuary,' while the rest of the unit would serve as the parsonage where I or any future pastor could live. So I asked 'Papa' Curt how we could do that. He said, "We'll put the Title in the name of '**YAH** Gives A Second Chance Ministry.'" And that is exactly what we did. So if I die, The ministry would continue under a believing heart in the blood of Yahshua the Messiah. Although I don't say he's my 'father' lightly. I say it because in my heart he is. He and his wife treat me like I belong to them.

On one of their visits to see me 'Papa Curt' was working on my computer at the desk of my shop, so I started combing his (long) hair, making braids and putting rubber bands on them as I had done to my real father. This was not unusual for him because his daughters used to do exactly the same thing to his hair. When a friend came and saw what I was doing, although other people were in the shop, her mouth dropped open. I thought she was shocked that I was able to braiding a white man's hair. After that day she treated me differently, even getting totally nervous whenever I came around. I prayed and asked "**Father Yah'uah** "What did I -do to her?" He showed me the whole scene in my head. What had happened in my shop? So I called her and asked her and she said that it had bothered her. So I thought to myself, what really bothered her was that a white man and his wife had purchased the mobile home for the ministry and a place for me to live, a place where I could help people. But she made me feel unclean. So I called 'Papa' Curt's wife, Gretchen, and I questioned her about it. She explained to me that some people might not understand my relationship with pop Curt; I asked her plainly, did she believe I was trying to manipulate her husband in any way. She said no, but she said she was uncomfortable with it because it is something another woman shouldn't do. I was thinking, "I'm not another woman, I am his daughter." And I said to her that it never entered my mind because it is something I always did whenever my father would come to see us. Black people always comb each other's hair. I did not understand how they got something sexual out of that. From that day on I have been afraid to be close to 'Papa' Curt because I did not want anyone to think that I did something wrong with him. He is not that kind of person; 'Papa' Curt is totally faithful and devoted to his wife. They are an ongoing story of two people deeply in love, they always seeming to me to be just 'falling in love.' They always have that feeling of unity with each other. A few days later I asked him about his response to criticisms of the incident of our relationship and he said, "I never thought anything unusual was implied by what you did that day because I've always thought of you as my own daughter!" I thought to myself. I belong to a family. No wonder he had allowed me to braid his hair and why I've always felt he was my true 'papa.'

I ended my friendship with the woman because she didn't really understand or trust me and most people don't. To me people like her always want to say "I'm better than you." They're looking for something to accuse another person with, even when they know the other person is innocent. When you have a lot of guilt within you, the world seems guilty of everything you would do, so you don't see the purity of others. She was a friend I lost. The loss of a friend is like going to a funeral. You've buried them; it is a waste to look back at what you used to have; now you move on. Tomorrow can be a whole new beginning and can bring new friends. People are always getting new friends, but an old friend who can be trusted is hard to find for me. A friend is better than a glass of fine wine. That friend gets better with age. There are very few long-term friends: people's friendships seem to be based on emotions rather than on facts and neutral trust and respect.

After I wrote this story of my life, the woman and I were able to talk about what had really happened and our precious friendship has been restored! Was Father Yah'uah in this friend? He was. I didn't really understand *HER MOTIVES OR UNDERSTOOD HER HURT'S*

My Move to Hinesville, Georgia

Now I will tell you how I get to Georgia? I came here to visit Margaret. While visiting her I fell in love with this place. I am a born New Yorker. I've been to Germany. I've been to Africa. In those places I went to by myself and in only one of them did I know anybody. As I said earlier I had become a drug dealer using the money to help others; I didn't have the concept that I was saving some and killing others. Selling drugs means you have money; having money means you have power to do whatever you want to do. I wanted to help people; selling drugs was the only way I knew how to get money to bring change in people's lives. I was not trying to change them for the worse. I wanted something better for them; I never had anyone to show me how to do that. So I did what I had seen done all of my life for people to have money. I sold drugs to take care of people. And on the other hand I was destroying the same people I wanted to 'save.' It is ironic how Satan can cloud your mind. He can make you think wrong is right.

Confrontation by the 'Lord'

The last time I had come to Georgia to visit was on a Saturday. On Sunday morning every channel on television had a preacher preaching. I love television, so I had to look at it. The preacher was saying, "Give your life to 'Jesus.'" Something happened to me that day. I began to cry out like I had never cried before. There was no explanation why I was crying. Everything in me was hurting; everything in me was saying, "'Jesus,' 'Jesus' come into my life because I know I can't change me. I want to know you. If you are real then change me. I don't know how to find you. So you've got to find me. Please 'Jesus,' just come into my life; find me. I cannot do this anymore; I just cannot live like this." That night I took heart medicine, at least 15 pills from that one bottle; I also took high blood pressure medicine, at least 20 from that one bottle. I took 30 tablets of painkillers and some 'black beauties.' And I lay on the couch. I heard someone calling my name. I heard someone say, "Get up, Prayer Warrior Gloria." I was in that house by myself but I know I heard that voice. I did not get up. Someone' pulled me up by my hand. When I turned around to see who was there, there was no one there but me. I never threw up. I never got sick and I never had my stomach pumped. A miracle had taken place, and I knew 'Jesus Christ' the Messiah was there. I 'died' that night and came back to life with a sense that 'God' had a purpose for me. I gave my life to 'Jesus' in that room that night. Only I was there, crying out to 'Jesus' to show me how to live for him.

But I really did not trust him yet. I had fallen down, lots of times but every time I did he was still standing there, waiting to pick me up again He had to pick me up so many times and to keep telling me that he was not the enemy, but I had not gotten it yet. I could hear His voice inside of me saying, "You're still in the race." There were lots of times I failed, but he would not let me go. But it took some work and years to help me let go of the past. This is the last straw. I have to put on the altar. Every time he would pick me up I would allow people to say things to me that would cause me to shut down on the Messiah. I wanted the people to love me and accept me, but some of them could not. I wanted to love them but I did not know how and I could not. To me love was a nasty word. It was full of sex and hurt. So I thought, "Who needs it?"

I knew how to deal with hate, anger, distrust, lying, fighting, partying, and manipulating, but I didn't know how to deal with love. I had to learn how to love and how to trust people. But first I had to stop being so angry with myself and with everybody else. I was a

Person not an animal and no one's property I had to believe that "*Yah'shua*" the Messiah died for me and I was part of his family, something I never really had. After years of abuse, the only place that I felt like I belonged was with "*Yah'shua*." But still I did not fully trust him. I wanted him in my life. I knew he was good for me, but I just couldn't give him full charge over me. One of the hardest things was to allow people to touch my skin and hug me. And I would hurt every time I heard the name 'Jesus' ("*Yah'shua*"), but I was determined to please 'God' ("**Father Yah'uah**" *Elohim*). I did not want to lose Him, but I was still skeptical of 'Jesus' ("*Yah'shua*"). I would say with my mouth that I wanted 'Jesus' in my life. But in reality, I only wanted 'God' (**"Father Yah'uah"** *Elohim*) the Father, without the Son. I wanted the church, but not the people.

My First Church

The first church I went to was an all-black church. They did a lot of outreach work. The pastor was worldly, but his wife was 'godly.' He knew about 'Jesus' ("*Yah'shua*"), but that was not how he lived; she knew about 'Jesus' and that is how she lived. He mistreated his wife, but she stayed faithful to him. I was so angry that I couldn't stand to even look at him. Why was she so faithful to him when he was doing craziness to her? He would belittle her in front of the congregation, speak evil of her, and flirt with other women. But yet she continued to pray for him in the church. I remembered that night on the couch when I heard 'Jesus' ("*Yah'shua*") say "Prayer Warrior Gloria." I really thought He meant a fighting warrior. You know, like beating somebody down. Whenever the pastor said something to me, I would say something ugly to him. One day he said something harsh in front of the church about his wife. I waited until he was alone, and then I said to him, "You have a good wife; but if I had been her, I would have left you a long time ago!" I never said much to him after that, because every time he had a chance he would say negative things to me. He said, "If you knew how to read, you would understand why I treat her like that. I'm just putting her in her place. I am the head of this church. In my house whoever doesn't like it can leave." So I left the church. At that time I did not know how to pray or what was the proper way to speak to the pastor. I needed to allow "**Father Yah'uah**" to still allow the Holy Spirit to teach me. I still had a lot of fight in me if someone did something to me. I would say in my mind Jesus Yahshua the Messiah hold my coat while I go handle them. I definitely need more guidance from Father Yah'uah. I just did whatever came into my mind, but most of the time whatever came into my mind was wrong. I was still fighting people. Now they were not in Mama's house; they were in the church. I did not know how to follow leadership; everyone who had been leaders in my life had failed me. So I was not about to let anyone tell me what to do, especially not some man who had total control over everybody in the congregation. To me that was crazy, but **"Father Yah'uah"** was patient with me. He knew I did not understand how to follow a leader. I would learn that from Pastor Dicky Welch.

My Second Church

My next church was an all-black church too. It was one of the most powerful churches in Hinesville. The people were herded like they were horses and the cowboy was taming them. Everything that the people did had to be approved by the pastor. If a man wanted to take his wife out, he had to have permission from his pastor. If you wanted to change jobs or move away, you had to have permission from the pastor. If you wanted to buy your family a new house, you had to have permission from the pastor. I did not know that one man could have that much control he had control over people like Mama had in her house. That kind of control reminded me of Mama. He said to me, "Why do you resist me so much?" I told him I did not understand a lot that went on in church families. He said, "You just stay here and you will learn what to do." At that time I still could not read, but I always had lots of questions. My son, Darlus, had been murdered around that time of year. The pastor said to me, "You need to be in counseling." I wanted 'God' (**"Father Yah'uah"** *Elohim*) so badly I would've done anything he told me to, yet I was still afraid of "*Yah'shua*" the Messiah. So I began going to counseling. When Darlus died I never cried. I would only talk if you were talking to me and I was working on something with you. Other than that, I had nothing to say. I made the mistake of telling the pastor some of the things that had been done to my brothers and sisters and me. It was the biggest mistake I had ever made. I wanted 'God' (**"Father Yah'uah"** *Elohim*) to help me to forgive my mama and to forgive those who had killed my son. Yet I could also feel the hatred that was coming out of me towards people. I looked calm to them, but on the inside I was steaming. I was boiling completely over, and I was going to stop anybody who got in my way no matter how I had to do it. I was not going to give anyone control over my life. Nobody would have a chance to force me to do anything I said "no" to; that included the pastor.

Entrepreneurship

The money that I got from my son's insurance policy went to open a bookstore called Darlus Religious Arts. But before I go any further, I have to explain something first. I had no formal background in religion, not about **"Father Yah'uah"** *Elohim* who is God or His son *"Yah'shua the Messiah"* who is Jesus Christ or the adversary Satan—no religious teaching except for my sister 'Hot Mama' teaching me the 23rd Psalm. Just about every corner store in Brooklyn had stores that sold all kinds of things that I thought were to help people do better. Christian people would leave church and go there and buy things like Lucky House Spray, Indian Money House Spray, Big Money House Spray, good luck oil, Juju oil, Bibles, "How to Get Your Lover Back" and all kinds of things that deals with spells so that their husbands would not leave them. Then there were candles of every color you can imagine, lucky number books, voodoo books, crosses, rosaries, and many other such things. I saw Christian people come out of their church, go across the street, and buy these things. So I thought they were Christian things. I called one of my friends in Brooklyn, New York and asked her to go to the store and ask the people how to order the stuff because she had a friend who wanted to open up a store like that. When she sent the paper to me, I took it straight to the pastor and asked the cowboy what he thought. I wanted to know if he thought it would be a good business for me to open up. He asked me, "What did 'God' tell you to do?" I did not know 'God' told you to do certain things like open up a store; I thought He only told you to do stuff like don't be mean to His people. I just wanted to create a business so I could help take care of people. I no longer wanted to take care of people with drug money. I wanted my own income so I would not have to depend on any other person to take care of me. After I received the insurance money I gave the church a check for my tithe and an offering of $400. I did not understand that I had stepped into things that weren't of "**Father Yah'uah**" *Elohim*. In my heart I believe the pastor let me do this as a punishment, because I challenged so much of what he said, things like, "If your pastor asked you to walk down the street buck naked, would you do it?" Everyone else in that class said yes. I said "no." When the man who was teaching the class asked me why I said no, I said, "Because he's just a man like everybody else in here." He said, "I'm using this as an example," and I said, "I'm answering you as an example." I was not trying to be smart. I was telling him what I really thought. He said to me, "You have to learn that whatever your pastor tells you to do, you have to do that." What was going on in my head at that time? I was thinking either I was crazy or they were. His next example to me was, "If your pastor tells you to walk off the edge of a roof would you?" My answer was still "no." I was thinking while I'm land in my grave. I would say that was dumb. The next Tuesday I wasn't allowed in the classroom anymore. Whenever the people went to the altar, they would be on one side and I would be on the other. They would not even allow anyone to sit on the same bench with me. But I didn't know that the pastor had given that order and they did not know that the pastor said it was okay for me to buy those items for the store. Over the years I have watched him be punished for what he did to different people who belong to the powerful house of "**Father Yah'uah**" *Elohim.*

When I went to my first pastor's wife, she said, "Love covers a multitude of sin," and, "The truth will come out one day. Just be! Patient" The truth never came out. People had already begun calling me a witch and a prostitute; everything I had told him in that room he and that lady who was in the room told the entire church. A little child said to me, "I am not supposed to speak to you. My dad said you are a witch and a prostitute." I asked him in front of his parents if he knew what those words meant. He replied no he did not" but he knew I was bad. No one was telling me why except for that child. The adults all thought I was coming against the church with witchcraft prayer and trying to get their husbands. It would be one year later that an old lady came in my store and asked me, "'Baby,' do you know what all the things in this store are used for?" I said to her, "No, I do not." She asked me why I bought the stuff and I told her my pastor said it was okay. She said, "'Baby,' everything in here is for the work of Satan had Father Yah'uah sent that old woman to minister to me? She said if you love 'Jesus' our 'Lord' and Savior, close this store." I was so upset with the pastor. He knew I did not know what was good and what was bad. I really wanted to fight with him. I would've started a fight but I did not want 'Jesus' or 'God' to be mad at me. So I was trying not to fight with him.

I asked 'Jesus' if He would teach me how to read. I did not want anybody else to tell me what was right or wrong. I wanted to read the word of 'God' by myself. I called a friend of mine to go by me a gallon of 'Johnny Walker Red.' I locked myself up in my house and I started praying and drinking and smoking. My Marlboro cigarettes the next day I went and closed the store. I didn't hear from 'God' to do that, I just did it. The store was named Darlus Religious Arts in honor of my son. So when I had to close it, it was another thing that broke my heart; but because I wanted a true relationship with "*Yah'shua*", I let it go. There was no retaliation on my part against the pastor. I had made up my mind purposefully to close it. I was going to know "*Yah'shua*" the Messiah for myself. Even to this very day people mistreat me because of the bookstore. I never once made it public what the pastor had purposely misled me, but I watched the things that happened in his life. It was as though 'God' justified me. Yet I still did not know that I did not have to fight my own battles. That was the job of the Messiah. It is funny to me now how we say, "'God,' take control of my life." But when someone does anything to us we say, "Hold my coat while I handle them, 'Jesus.'" I knew I could fight, but somehow I did not want to.

I still could not read, so I locked myself up with my gallon of 'Johnny Walker Red' and began trying to remember the words 'June Bug" had taught me. Sesame Street came on television while I was cleaning one day. Every word that was flashed on the television set I remembered. I would see it later on and automatically know what the word was. The more I watched Sesame Street, the more I learned. When I would run out of my liquor, my friend Robin would go get me more of my gallon of 'Johnny Walker Red' and my cart of Marlboro cigarettes At first I would read my Bible while I smoked my cigarettes and drank my 'Johnny Walker Red.' Then I found myself standing by the door smoking and drinking my next drink next I would go in the bathroom and smoke and take my drink. Then it was always outside of the door. Then I just stopped drinking and smoking for about 3 years. But after that, whenever I got extremely upset because 'God' would not let me fight His people who got me extremely upset, I would always go back to drinking and smoking. Did I have a drinking problem? No, I did not. I had a past problem. That is how I had handled all of my problems in the past—I would drink and go dancing and not think about anything else.

Probably somewhere deep inside of me, I did not want to let the Messiah have total control over my life. Yes, I still would harbor anger, hatred and madness. I was still seriously ill in my thoughts and in my heart, but I tried to master all of it so no one would know but me. I would add it to the long list of abuse that went on in my life. So the connection that I wanted with 'Jesus' (*"Yah'shua"*) the Messiah had not yet come I knew His 'name.' I knew who he was, but I did not really know him. It was now going on 5 years that I had been a Christian. I wasn't fighting people physically, but mentally I was. I got my first DUI and I was spinning more and more out of control if someone got me angry. I would go home and damage some of the house because I could not get to fight that person. I felt like 'God' ("**Father Yah'uah**" *Elohim*) was protecting them and he loved them more than me. So they could do anything they wanted to me, but I could not fight his precious children. I understand now why not, but I did not understand then. Praise to the Name of "**Father Yah'uah**" *Elohim* for the protection of the blood of "*Yah'shua*" over each of his children. You can really see it in the story of King Saul and King David. [This story is found in 1 Samuel 16 through 2 Samuel 1. Saul, while king of Israel, became jealous of David because 'God' seemed to favor David over Saul. Although David remained loyal to Saul, Saul attempted to kill David.]

Service to Others

I had always taken other people's children in while I was in New York. I have cared for several children and teenagers since I've been in Georgia to. I have either helped them and their mothers work things out, or they have stayed with me and I have become a

Temporary mother for them I cared for a boy that we are going to call him 'Williams.' 'Williams' was a white child. I went to clean his mother's house because she was there sick. Some other Christian friends told me that she didn't have anybody to help her, so I went to clean her house without charging her anything. After cleaning and cooking for her and her kids, the children came home. The oldest child was a boy. His mother was saying she was going to put him up for adoption. There was so much anger in her voice. I went into her bedroom, keeping my head bowed low, and I asked her if I could talk to her for moment. I'm going to call her 'Brenda.' I kept my eyes cast down to the floor; I never looked up. I asked her, "If you are going to give your son up for adoption, please give him to me." She looked at me with shock and surprise on her face. She could not believe I was really asking her that question. I said to her, "Please, if you put him in the system you'll have a hard time trying to get your child back. But if you give him to me, when you're ready to have him back you can. I won't take any money from you. I'll just care for him." I gave her my telephone number and my address.

To my surprise, at nine o'clock the next morning she was at my house with 'Williams' and a brown paper bag half-filled with two shirts, one pair of underwear, and a pair of shorts. I did not have a telephone number for her. I just had the 10-year-old boy. The first thing that I did was I contacted Margaret and asked her as a friend, if she would help me with him. There were no strings attached to it. She agreed. Margaret never had children and she loved children. I asked her to start sending him letters in his mother's name and boxes of clothing and toys. I asked her to wire me $500 so I could make one of the rooms in my house comfortable for him. She did. I sat down with him and asked him if he would go to the store with me after school. He agreed. You could see in this child's face anger and fear, especially just being given to a total stranger, a black one at that. After school we went to Wal-Mart. I asked him to pick out a comforter, pillow and curtain that he liked. We also bought throw rugs, a television, a radio for his room, towels and washcloths, underwear, toothbrush and toothpaste, brush and comb, a couple of shirts, a couple of khaki pants, dress pants and shorts, two pairs of tennis shoes and one pair of dress shoes. Margaret gave me $500 and I used $300 of my own money. Then we went shopping for food that I knew a 10-year-old would prefer and things that he liked. He kept asking me if it was okay to get this or that or if he should put something back. I kept saying, "Just put it in the shopping cart." I allowed him to pick out three toys. The smile that was on his face was worth it all.

'Williams' went everywhere I did. I was home every day by the time he got out of school having a snack ready for him and his dinner that he said he wanted that day before going to school was being prepared for him. I hired some teenagers to help him with his homework after school. The highest mark he had received on the papers I saw from his school was a forty-nine, but this child was extremely intelligent. I knew something had happened to him and he was not telling it yet. I went to all his school meetings. I talked with his teachers. I told everyone the same story: his mother had left him with me to watch for her for a while until she found an apartment and a good job. I knew it was lying, but I did not know what to do to keep this child from going into the system and I did not want him to feel that no one loved him. I wanted him to know that somebody loved him. Even if they were black I even told 'Williams' that story, that his mother said she would be writing him. As soon as she got settled in Margaret started sending him letters as though she was his mother. I would ask him certain things he liked about his mother and things they had done together. And I would sit with him and tell him what to write back to his mother. He would ask her to call him in his letters. That was one thing we couldn't pull off. So I said to Margaret in her next letter to tell him she couldn't afford a telephone right now, and that worked. His birthday was coming up. Everything he wanted I had him put on paper and I sent it to Margaret. Everything including a bicycle was in his room when he came home from school. Margaret sent me the money by Western Union and he had a birthday party so he got to invite all of his friends from church.

The white people were getting upset with me at my church. His teachers at school were asking questions about his mother and if he liked living with a black lady. 'Williams' came home from school so upset. He told me everything that was said to him. I could not understand why they were so upset. He was clean and doing better in school. He started coming home with 100, 95. An A+ was it because a white child was living in a black woman's house and he was calling me "Mommy?" At church when 'Williams' got tired he would put his arms around my neck and lay his head on my chest or lay his head in my lap. Child protective services called on me, and Mr. Ron Walker paid me a house visit. I told him the mother had asked me to baby-sit for her. I showed him his school papers, and I told him she was sending me money to care for 'Williams.' But 'Brenda' had not given me any money at all. It had not been part of our agreement and I knew I was lying but I could not let this child suffer by going into force care he needed to know that someone cared about him he needed someone to fight for him I have asked Father Yah'uah to forgive me for lying I just didn't know what else to do. After Mr. Walker saw his room and his schoolwork from when he first came to be with me, he did not take the child from me. 'Williams' was bringing home A's and 100%'s on his work from school. He was so proud of himself, and when he had plays and things he would always look to see if I was there in the audience. That made me feel real good, because I had never gone to any activities for my children - not because I didn't love them, but because at that time all I could think about was making sure I had money coming in to take care of them. The lowest mark he came home with was 95. He was so proud of himself and I was proud of him too. He grew to love me and I loved him too; we needed each other to heal. He opened up to me.

When Williams first came to me he would put chairs by his bedroom door. He would not allow me to help him dress or sit on his bed. At first I thought he was afraid of black people. If he was in the bathroom and he forgot something, he would make me lay it outside of the bathroom door. If I needed something out of the bathroom, he would not allow me to come in and get it, even with the curtains closed. He was so afraid of me touching him. Sometimes if he did not see me coming he would jump when he saw me. I said to myself. I know I'm ugly, but not that ugly to make him jump. I knew all of those signs. So after school I began to talk to him about his day and the things that made him mad or upset. Then I gradually asked him things that he did not like people to do to him inappropriately. Tears began to stream down this child's face. And he said his mother's boyfriend had been doing things to him and making him do things with his sister. He said his mother didn't want him because of her boyfriend, but the boyfriend wanted her to keep the little girl. Those types of men always leave when the money runs out or they find another woman with new children for them to abuse. 'Williams' had been sexually and mentally, verbal abused. All of the signs were there. But other people had not seen them. 'Williams' was smart, and with the right love in his life this child could be anything he wanted to be. I began to pray that his real mother would call us. When she did call, I began to tell her all the things that 'Williams' had accomplished. She could not believe it. Children that are being abused don't always think very well. They are consumed with trying to please their parents are there abuser and wondering why their parents does not make it stop also they try to please the abuse, not because they want what they are doing to them, but because they think that somehow the abuser will stop or the abuser use threats to keep them in line if they continue to please them. They will be safe. Most of the time it is difficult for them to think. It is as though their minds are always somewhere else. I told Williams mother. Everything that had happened to her child I also told her what Margaret and I had done so she would know what to talk to him about and she could ask him if he liked the things she sent him. It worked out. 'Williams' lived with me for about two years. I asked her not to talk to him about the child abuse until he was home with her. This way she could understand her child's feelings and find a way to deal with this situation. That would leave him feeling whole.

One day his mother came and said she wanted her child back. That was a happy time for me because his mother saw the value of her child. At the same time, 'Williams' had an older brother who started calling my house. I believe he was in college. He thanked me for what I had done for his brother. 'Brenda' gave me a plaque that reads, "Dreams are made to come true. The Heart of Christ,' 1991that plaque stayed in a box packed away until I got to this triple-wide trailer. Now it is on my front door. After telling the biological mother of 'Williams' all he had told me that the man had done to him, I told her she should find the proper authorities so that 'Williams' would not be scarred for life. Since he left me he has called me twice. I told his mother to listen to the things her child had to say, and they would do well. She said to me, "I never met anyone like you; people like you don't exist." She said I was a 'black angel.' I would hear those same words later on in my life from another white person. The next day when he left, everything that was in his room went with him, all his awards, his clothing and toys and his bedding. That gave him peace to have his things in his new home with him. He wanted a picture of me but I said no because I did not want him to have a reminder that his mother left him with a stranger someone black that he did not know. The next child I would keep had a father who was in the military. A girlfriend of mine brought the father to meet me and to pray for their relationship. The next thing I knew the father was asking me to take care of his child until he got back from Iraq. He said he would be gone about a year. The boy was four years old. His father was African and he had no family here. I took the child but his father never gave me any money for him, not one thing. He only called him once. I got in touch with Margaret again. She wanted me to report the father to the Army. I explained to her that 'God' had trusted me with 'Freddy.' (This was not his real name, but this is what I'll call him.) I said to her, "I'm doing all of the things I never did with my own children." So, she helped me again. She started sending boxes of clothing, toys, and other things. She made sure he believed his father was sending him cards and letters. She was real good at that. Before his father left him with me, he gave me $2,500. He said it was for him to get paperwork done for his son so he could get full custody of him and he would be able to stay in the United States. He asked me to put it up for him. When he came back, I gave him every penny of his money. I kept it in his son's bedroom closet locked in a box. The father was a private in the Army trying to save money to get an apartment and to get the necessary things for himself and his son to start a new life when he came back to the United States. I had helped a lot of privates in the Army so one more didn't really matter.

Every day Margaret is in my prayers. I ask "**Father Yah'uah**" *Elohim* to help her find herself and to give her life to *"Yah'shua."* I believe in my heart that some day she will, but in "**Father Yah'uah**" *Elohim*'s time. He has an appointed time. "For He says: 'In an acceptable time I have heard you, and in the day of salvation I have helped you. Behold, now is the accepted time; behold, now is the day of salvation.' "

(2 Cor.6: 2) He says, "Come on in now." Some of us accept the call. Some of us refuse to come in at all, so we choose death rather than life and assign ourselves to the evil one and hellfire where Satan can devour us.

"**Father Yah'uah**" is calling some of you. Just say, "'Jesus' (*"Yah'shua"*), come into my life and my mind. I don't know how to do things the right way anymore but I am tired of doing them the wrong way. I am tired of having to do it alone." There is a way out by laying down all of it at the feet of The Messiah *"Yah'shua,"* at the foot of his stake ('cross'). He is our deliverer.

Lisa and Lewis

The last baby I cared for I am going to call 'Anna' I met the entire family through the sister-in-law of the mother. We are going to call her 'Lisa' and the father 'Lewis.' 'Lisa' already had one baby. She was thinking about having an abortion because she and her boyfriend at the time were struggling to care for the first baby. The father, 'Lewis', was a heavyset young man. 'Lewis' was such a joy to be around. He would eventually marry 'Lisa' and start a business, and they both gave their lives to "*Yah'shua*" the Messiah. 'Lewis' had such a good heart. If he was around you, he would find something to make you laugh about. I called him my son and 'Lisa' my daughter. 'Lisa' had been abused as a child, and she was adopted. She had a brother who was in jail. She had no family here in Georgia besides the family of 'Lewis', so when she found out she was pregnant for the second time she thought she could not raise another child without a husband. She thought of having an abortion because she felt she could not raise another child by herself. She had tried to abort the baby by herself. When she said that to me I begged her not to have an abortion I said, "I will help you with the baby." So she had the baby. I would drive from Hinesville to Glennville and help her with the baby.

One day she called me, crying and saying it was too much for her to take care of two small children by herself. She wanted to get a job and go to school, so one of my volunteers, Major R. Ellyson, and I went to pray with her. I asked her if I could bring the baby back to Hinesville with me; she said yes. I did it for the weekend and then took her back to her mother. She stayed with her mother for a week. Then 'Lisa' called me again and asked me to take the baby. I said, "Let me keep the baby for you and when you want your baby back I will bring her to you." The baby was three months old, and she hollered the whole drive back to Hinesville. I was working at 'The Heart of Christ, Inc.'. The baby had to go to work with me every day. I would pack our stuff and off to work we went. I asked people through the newspaper in our community for a baby crib. This time it was a whole community helping me takes care of her. People would come into 'The Heart of Christ, Inc.' and say, "Where is the baby?" They would always have a prayer or something beautiful for her. Up until she was five years old, one lady would bring her new clothing. Used things were always donated to us. She had all kinds of toys to play with. She was loved by everyone, regardless of nationality or race. They would come just to see her. She had her own corner at my workplace, where I had a refrigerator and a hot plate. We had it made—all the love that I could give her I did.

I did not know how to give my love to my Monique. Because I did not know how or what I had missed by not giving my own daughter my love, it made me feel bad how I had denied my real daughter my love. I was not afraid to give this baby a bath by myself, and I was not afraid I might do something inappropriate to her. I was confident that I was being what a mother was supposed to be. She was three years old the first time I left her with someone else other than her mother. That was with my daughter Monique, when Monique came to visit me. When 'Anna' woke up and did not see me, she gave my Monique a run for her money. Monique called me and said, "Mommy, come and get your baby because my sister won't stop crying. You better come home now." I laughed all the way home and got my baby.

When 'Lisa' wanted her baby to come home to her, her real mother, the baby would cry to come back to me. She loved her mother; she also loved me. The baby would not stay with her real mother long. 'Lisa' got mad at me. She came to get her on two occasions. The baby screamed and hollered so badly that they put her out of the car, and she ran straight into my arms. One day 'Lisa' and her sister-in-law and her brother-in-law came to get the baby. They did not even call me. When she came to take her, 'Anna' had a tantrum. It was so emotional for all of us. I asked 'Lisa' to let me bring her after work. She was yelling and screaming at me. I could not make out a word. She was say. The next thing I knew I had slammed her against the wall. I could hear her brother-in-law saying, "Don't do this. You are not supposed to put your hand on anyone." I had not wanted to hurt 'Lisa' or anyone else. I think the screaming and yelling and her approaching me in an aggressive manner caused the reaction to come out of me. I could hear him say, "Gloria, let 'Lisa' go." The next thing I knew, she had pulled out a large knife. I automatically went into a fighting stance. I grabbed the broom and hit her hand to make her drop the knife. When she did, I was going to fight her. I just kept saying, "Get the baby out of here," because she was crying and reaching for me and

I knew at that moment in time whatever happened was going to happen. I was not going to back down. I felt like the three of them came to start that fight. They just didn't know I would fight them back.

I would never start a fight after I became an adult. But I wouldn't let anyone hit me. If I could walk away from a fight I did, but if people did not give me room to get out of their way then it was trouble and I would let them know they were in for a fight. If I could talk to people to defuse a fight I would, but if you gave me no choice then I was not going to back down. I had taken *'tae kwon do'* classes, because I went in the woods to feed the homeless. Lots of times it would be just me and my clients would be men and young boys; sometimes it would be women. Most of my clients who lived in the woods were homeless men, who had some mental problems or were on drugs, so I had to have a way of defending myself if it ever came to that. It never did. Was Father Yah'uah in the woods with me? Yes, he was

'Lisa' was accusing me of trying to steal her baby. I had taken care of children most of my life and had always given them back to the parents. I loved 'Anna', but she belonged to 'Lisa'. 'Anna' had been with me so long that we got really attached to one another. 'Lewis' came and talked to me and said, "Gloria, don't be mad at my wife. It hurts her to know her baby loves you so much and she knows how good you have been to us. I love you and my wife does too for all the things in our house that you gave to us. You've taken care of our daughter and not asked us for one penny.

'Lisa' really appreciates what you've done for her and the baby. They are in the car. Can she come into your shop?" I said yes, because in my heart I loved them both. I used to tease the real grandmother and say, "I'm stealing your children and grandchildren." Ms. Louise would laugh at me because she knew I loved her son and her daughter-in-law.

'Lisa' came to me and apologized for her actions and I apologized for mine. Then we did a slow process of adjusting 'Anna' back to her mother. Their daughter had stayed with me for almost 6 years of her life. They had given me the most precious thing. 'Anna' brought me so much happiness and joy and peace with **"Father Yah'uah"** *Elohim*. I knew for sure I was nothing like my own mama, and **"Father Yah'uah"** could trust me with His gift. Another fear had died. It was laid at the feet of *"Yah'shua the Messiah,"* at His beautiful feet. When 'Lisa' had her third baby she named him after my son, Darlus.

'Lewis' and 'Lisa' are deceased now; 'Lewis' took both their lives. At their funeral I did not shed one tear, but inside I was screaming, "Somebody help me please somebody help me." I felt the same way that I felt when my twin sister died. I could not do anything to stop them from hurting her; I could not stop from hurting, so I started drinking and hiding it from people. It would be almost a month before I stopped. I could not talk to Father Yah'uah, not even to ask him why it had happened or why didn't he stop it. When *"Yah'shua"* draws you in, He begins to clean you and take away every fear. Sometimes it is within a blink of the eye, sometimes slow. But it is always sure. Your cleaning process may come with pain, but the end result is that you have peace with **"Father Yah'uah"** *Elohim* and man. Would my peace last long? No, I do not think so, because I still had secrets and lies to be told. Whenever you're covering up who you are, you are lying by saying, *"Yah'shua,"* I'm telling the truth." But the other hand is behind your back balled up tightly hiding your lie in waiting for the opportunity to fight. **"Father Yah'uah"** *Elohim* knows who you were and who you are supposed to be; He knows of your potential, because **"Father Yah'uah"** *Elohim* has created you to be who you are! And what he desires you to be.

Mental Health Care

During that time I met a lady named Misty Young from the mental health department. No one made me go to mental health; I simply thought I was crazy. She was the beginning of really coming home to *"Yah'shua"* the Messiah and finding me. I wanted to know how I got to the point that I could not feel any pain, could not remember names, and how I could totally forget people who I knew personally. What was it in me that caused that behavior? I would also totally forget whole situations. For instance, after my son died, I came home and I totally forget that he had died. Two years later I was waiting for him to call me. When someone asks me the date in October, the whole scene of his funeral plays back in my mind eye. I mean everything comes rushing back. I had a mild heart attack when it did come back to me. When I'm caring for someone and they're dying, and I know that they're dying, I shut down all emotional feelings towards them. I'm not cruel to them at all. I take care of them, feeding, and bathing them and getting up at night with them, and I stay with the family. But I get totally detached from the person. And when the family is in tears, screaming, hollering and mourning for the loss of their loved one, I get totally unemotional as though it's not happening, and I am wondering, "Why are they so upset?" There were other issues concerning me that I did not have answers for at that time.

I thought I was crazy. I had learned to protect myself and it was my primary goal not to let anyone hurt me. Misty the counselor said, "Gloria, you are not crazy but you only see black and white. You do not understand the gray areas." She wanted me to see Dr. Richard Anderson. He would drag out the dark areas of my life. He pulled me screaming and hollering out of the darkness that I had hidden within with the gentleness of a good friend, without drugs or medication of any sort, with just his words. He pointed me to who I really was. He was there, helping me all the way. He listened and he did not judge me. I had to keep from telling the whole truth to him. I was afraid if he knew everything I had done, he would stop talking to me. Now and then many of my secrets came out. He didn't judge me, he didn't curse me and he didn't even tell anyone about the dark things, the hideous things, the unbelievable things that I had done and that had been done to me. He told me because of the trauma in my life I had developed something called 'dissociation.' Many people who have been mistreated as children develop this kind of disorder. That is what Dr. Anderson explained to me. He also said there are different kinds of 'dissociation.' He gave me some books and I went to the library so I could understand what it was so I would know how to stop my radical behavior. I do not know if Dr. Anderson was a Christian I believe he was. I believe Father Yah'uah handpicked him to help me.

I will give you an example of 'dissociation.' My mama threw me out of a window once for not doing something with one of her clients. She also threw me out of the window because she caught me trying to read a book. I was reading out loud. She threw the book out of the window first, then me. So I was not able to read no matter how hard I tried. I was totally 'disassociated' from any form of reading. After I came to Hinesville, Georgia and 'Jesus' ("*Yah'shua*") came into my life and I asked 'God' ("**Father Yah'uah** *Elohim*) to help me, then I was able to read. But before that I could not read no matter how hard I tried even when June bug was trying to teach me I could not learn to read. Sometimes even now when I get extremely upset about something I forget how to read again.

I had to be all kinds of people for my mama's clients. I would have to be whomever they wanted me to be in order to take part in certain things. I had to think of myself as being someone else and that someone else was doing these things. I did not decide on having dissociation.' I had all of the characteristics of separating myself from any situation, including pain. I didn't think about separating myself, it just happened. So people at my son's funeral were thinking, "How can she not cry?" Once after having four hours of major surgery I got up and immediately walked out of the hospital. I wasn't thinking that I'd just had surgery. I just woke up, and I saw my stomach had been cut from the midway of my breasts past my navel. What I was thinking was that they cut me. So I left even though I knew I was supposed to have had an operation. I never think, "Today I'm not going to feel any pain;" it just happens. Right now I have an odor on my breath. It is some type of bowel blockage. The doctor to whom I was sent to get help for the problem began to yell at me because I asked too many questions. I don't know if I intimidated him but he felt like I'd asked him too many questions and he didn't have answers to them. So he began to speak to me harshly. It made me frightened to go back. Every time I try, panic sets in, or I totally forget to go because of the doctors who had hurt me in the past. So I either walk away from or won't go back to any type of aggression. Sometimes I am afraid for them. Because if I would decide to take a stance to stop them from whatever I think they are doing to me, that is wrong. I know I would use force. So if I stop talking or get quiet, I'm trying to save them or myself.

My doctor is probably one of the best doctors in our community. His whole staff has been extremely good to me. I had to have some B-12 shots. For months after the shots my arm hurt me. At the time the shots were given to me, I hollered out. The nurses thought I was being a baby about the shot. No, they were really hurting me. I could not move my arms or raise them. Even now when I try to lift my arms or turn a certain way, they hurt me. I know in my heart they were not trying to hurt me, but knowing it and trying to force myself to go back are two different things.

One of the dentists here in town I will call him Dr. J. When I first went to his office I had a toothache so bad I could not sleep or eat at all. This toothache was so extremely painful that I could not make the pain go away anymore. When I went to his office and sat in the chair my whole body started shaking violently. He stepped away from me. The shaking was so violent he put himself at a distance from me in the room. In the past I would go into a dentist's office to have some work done. They could not fix the problem, because I would have a seizure as soon as the dentist put his hand or anything into my mouth. But Dr. J. said to me, "I'm not going to touch you" and he was not upset with me for being frightened; he used a soft gentle voice to assure me. He meant me no harm. He said, "I'm going to send you home with a prescription. When you come back, bring someone with you. You take the medicine an hour before you come back to me." Afterwards his wife teased me sometimes. She said, "When you see me, you just say "Hi," but when you see my husband, you get the biggest smile on your whole face. You light up." I probably do because he didn't hurt me. He didn't tie me to a chair and beat me. He stepped away because he saw I was frightened. Because of him I now can go to any dentist without being afraid.

I hope you now have a good description of the work of **"Father Yah'uah"** *Elohim* and the people of my community who help me. Especially when I was trying to be as hard as nails and to act as normal as possible in order to keep my secrets hidden from everybody sometimes people or children would say to me, "How come you change your voice so often?" I did not realize that was happening to me. I did not want anyone to know I was different from them so I determined not to be close to anyone.

My Learning Style

I do not know why Christians, especially those who have the most power, are so afraid of everything. So I just don't tell anyone that I hear 'voices' telling me what to do, because I try my very best to make people feel comfortable around me. I do not want anyone to think I am crazy. Years later I started going to night school at Bradwell Institute in Hinesvilles to get my GED. [General Educational Development is coursework and testing in five subjects giving a diploma equivalent to a high school diploma]. At school one of the teachers did an example of division. I watched how she did the example. She wrote two more examples on the board. She called different people to do the examples. No one got the right answer but me. When she asked me how I got the answer, I could not explain to her. I did exactly what I saw her do, and the 'voice' in my head helped me to do the rest of it. That is how I do most of the things I do, simply by listening or watching or seeing an image, then I hear the voice say, "You can do it." I cannot hear how words sound, they don't have sounds to me; once I see them I know them.

I looked at Sesame Street, and they were showing a lot of different words. I prayed and asked **"Father Yah'uah"** if He could teach me to read; from that day on I was reading. Then Col. Brenda Mason paid for me to take college courses in religious arts, and Deborah Tunnage and her husband, children, and her mother-in-law, as well as Maj. Ronald Ellyson and Robert and Lydia Clark, began to work with me. So I learned to read by watching

Sesame Street and by listening to them, then hearing the voices tell me the rest of what I was supposed to do. It was what I heard in my head that helped me to understand and to choose right answers. Whenever I take a test that has multiple-choice questions I always score very high because I'm able to see the words and just fill in those round circles. So if people ask, "How did you pass that test if you can't spell?" I say that I didn't have to spell! I am able to read almost anything I see; that is how I received my driver's license. I get extremely nervous when I'm around other people, so sometimes I'm not able to read at all especially if I am being yelled at or I feel threatened. I become afraid that they think I do not understand, so I do nothing.

I remember once I was at Mrs. Deborah Tunnage's house. Her daughter was having a problem orienting the text in a file on her computer. I went over to her and said, "I know how to fix it." There was another lady behind me and I could see her out of the corner of my eye, waving her hands as if to say to her not to let me touch that computer. Some other people tried to orient the text and they could not fix it. I waited until everyone gave up, and then I went over and oriented the text. She had wanted to put it into landscape, but she did not know how to do it.

Most people do not give me any credit at all; they think I am a total moron, so that's how they treat me. In turn, I stay clear of people most of the time. Dr. Fraser allowed me to take a nurse's assistant's class at Fraser's Counseling Center. Everyone else thought I could not handle the class and that the class was too advanced for me, but I knew I could do it.

My School Experience

I had worked as a nurse's assistant in New York. They only paid me for seven hours a day, but I worked twenty-four hours. I lived in Ms. Leavitt's house and I had no vacation time off and no holidays, but they only paid me for seven hours. No one ever came to give me time off. I had worked with her for three years and then stopped. I really liked Ms. Leavitt, who was an elderly 'Jewish' woman. I knew as a child what a 'Jewish' couple had done to help me, so I worked for her as long as I could. Her daughter offered me more money to stay because no one wanted to take care of her. Whenever I left the room so she couldn't see me she would get upset.

I paid Ms. Rodriguez to take care of my children. My children had to come to my job to visit me sometimes. They spent some nights at Mrs. Leavitt's house. I was afraid for them because they had to ride the bus so far just to see me. I had to quit so they would not have to travel so far away by themselves.

With Margaret being overseas again, I wanted to go to school. I knew if Margaret was home she would not let me go to school. She would give upset sometimes whenever I tried to work or read by myself. I believe she was trying to protect me from anyone making fun of me or me hurting someone if they made me upset. After being cooped up in the house for two years I decided I was going to go to school to become a nurse's assistant.

Lots of times I imprisoned myself by not going outside unless it was absolutely necessary or if I had a job to go to. I had found work in a hospital in Brooklyn as a dietitian's assistant. All that means is that a dietitian fixed the food and I helped to put it on a tray.

I signed up for the program at Fraser's Counseling Center. Dr. Fraser allowed me to take these courses, even though people said I was not capable of attending or understanding the work. At school I was doing my work and helping a lot of the girls with their work and even giving them the right answers. One of the girls got mad at me once because she thought I had given her the wrong answers but I had not. Later they found out they had passed the tests, but then they told Mrs. Diane Carter I had cheated. Some girls were taking tests to become registered nurses and I would help them also with the right answers.

Three months before signing up for the class I started getting all kinds of books on nursing and nursing assistants as well as books on sign language. I also borrowed CDs on nursing and on sign language. Ms. Janie at Live Oak Church of 'God' also helped me with sign language. I read and got tapes and CDs on everything I could get my hands on concerning nursing. I did this because I knew I would be slower than the other students, so by the time I registered for class I was halfway ready for it all. Then the 'voices' in my head helped me to understanding the material a lot.

Sometimes I would sit quietly and visualize what something is supposed to look like. I would automatically know what to do. Once while at Fraser's Counseling Center the staff and Ms. Diane thought I had been cheating and someone else was doing my work. They put me in a room by myself and gave me some paperwork to do and they put a time clock in the room with me. I asked them if they would remove the clock. I would finish the thirty questions they gave me as quickly as possible. And I did; they were surprised I had every question right. None of the other girls had to do that test. If I had failed it they would have put me out of the program. Every step of the way the 'voices' in my head helped me to understand the questions that I was reading. When they asked me if I was lying about not having any real schooling, I said I was not lying to them. Ms. Diane Carter and I were always picking on each other. But there was something about her: I knew in my heart that she was not the enemy, she just wanted the girls to do their very best and for none of us to fail. She was hard on us and I challenged her all the time. When she told me to do something that I thought was unreasonable or unfair, I 'gave her hell.' But she somehow saw something in me that I could not see, and she was determined to pull it out of me. She once said to me, "Gloria, you have the potential to help a lot of people and to help them go a long way." Today I can say I truly love Ms. Diane Carter. She did not want to break my spirit; she only wanted to shape it in me. Was Father Yah'uah in the staff of Fraser's counseling center? He was especially in Ms. Diane Carter.

My Trip to Africa

When I went to Germany for two years I met a lot of Africans. They were not allowed to move around as freely as myself. I would give them food and clothing because most of them did not have good jobs, but they were happy to be there in Germany. Their only concern was to get money to send back to Africa to take care of their families. The basic things they did not have. The majority of them lived cramped up in one room. I believe if people do not have the basic things to take care of themselves, they will steal food, clothing, and other things they need. So I try to eliminate that effect in their lives. And when you are helping people and showing them better ways to live and giving them the basic things you eliminate most of the problems, and you give them hope. They tend to want to work and gain self-respect and want even better things for their lives and their children's. I have seen that in so many different cultures.

I had a recurring nightmare; I would be running through a forest in Africa and a man with a spear would throw it and stab me in my side. Then I would look up and see trees that reached up to the sky and bits of sunlight shining through them. I would stumble to the edge of the cliff and fall off. I would always wake up at that part. I would be frightened, terrified, sweating, breathing hard, and not able to think clearly. I did not know why I was having that dream but I did know I was determined to see

Africa. I asked Margaret to help me help the African people with things they needed. Whatever I needed for them Margaret made sure I had, things like toothpaste, deodorant, clothing, underwear, coats, jackets, hats, boots, shoes, sneakers, gloves; and whenever they needed money to travel with I made sure they had it, no matter how much. Margaret would fuss with me because there would be so many African people in the house. When Margaret got home from work she never fussed with me because she thought I was doing something wrong she fussed with me because they took up all my time. She knew I was always taking care of people, babies, or animals. She had gotten used to that, although she would say, "Gloria, you cannot take care of the world."

I woke up crying one day and Margaret asked me what was wrong. I said, "I want to go to Africa." She replied, "You don't know anything about Africa, Gloria. And they live much differently than we do." I said, "They are just people like us. We are in Germany, and I have so many friends – Germans, Africans, Americans, and some people from Thailand who could not speak English or German, but we found a way to communicate with them." I had made friends with all kinds of people. And I was not afraid of going to a strange country, so I thought, "I will be fine." I would be just fine. Because so many different people came to Mama's house I was not afraid of strange people of different ethnic backgrounds. I have been around strange people all my life and people from different ethnic backgrounds. To me it would be just like going to another part of Brooklyn and I would be on a great adventure. She said that the people have different languages. But I knew in my heart that I would be fine. She said few people spoke English and I would have a difficult time; she was afraid for my safety, so her answer was "No." So I started going out to nightclubs, dancing until the clubs closed, coming home and drinking until morning. Margaret finally said, "You can go to Africa, Gloria."

When I got there I was supposed to stay in a hotel. Some of the African people I had met in Germany had their family members meet me at the airport. I was in Ghana, West Africa. All of them wanted to take care of me, but the one who stood out the most to me was Pee; he was a young man named Pee. Pee was still in school. He was one of the best mannered and polite young teenagers I had ever met since I'd left home, meaning Brooklyn, New York. People I had never met wanted to take care of me, plus Pee could speak English pretty well. He would be my bodyguard and my interpreter.

My first night there I found out where the nightclub was, so I went dancing and partied as usual. All night Pee waited for me outside until the club closed. It didn't take them long to find out that I was not from Africa. I had a great time that night so instead of Pee taking, me back to the hotel he took me to his village and to his parents' house. He thought I was too friendly plus I was from America, so he thought someone would take advantage of me. When I woke up I was wrapped in a sheet. His mother and sister had taken my clothes off and washed them by hand, I mean everything. He had waited until I got up before going into my purse and getting the key to my hotel room so he could get my suitcases and my clothing later on that day. They wrapped me in African dress clothing and headdress. As you have realized I was still 'Miss Worldly World.' I did whatever I thought I was big enough to do. The dream had been just part of why I wanted to go to Africa; I wanted to know how to help people to obtain their goals in life.

Concepts of Good and Bad

I really thought black magic and white magic and Christianity were all the same thing, because I had no background in any of them and no one had yet explained to me the differences. I thought that if some people were 'evil' they were just mean and bad, like Mama. I thought if some were 'good,' then 'God' loved them. If you were 'good' you went to 'heaven,' and if you were 'bad' you went to 'hell.' You would have to be stealing or drinking too much whiskey, and you would have to be sleeping with other ladies' husbands, and then you would go straight to 'hell.' If you were a 'good' woman, then 'God' loved you because you were helping people do better, and so you went to 'heaven.' If a man did not spend all his money playing cards, drinking whiskey, and chasing women he was a 'good' man and 'God' loved him and he could go to 'heaven.' But if he slept with a lot of women, played cards and drank a lot of whiskey, and didn't take care of his household, then he was going straight to 'hell.' That is exactly what I thought; that was the limit of my knowing about 'heaven' and 'hell,' and 'good' and 'evil.' There was only a thin line in my thinking, because it was limited to my surroundings and my understanding of 'good' and 'evil.' There was not any difference between Christianity and 'black magic' to me; these things were what you did if you wanted 'God' to love you. I wanted 'God' to love me, but I did not want 'Jesus' to love me; He was bad. I wanted to learn all I could about 'black magic.' I wanted to be like "Bewitched" on television. She was always doing something good and making people laugh, and I wanted to be just like her. Television was my only source for knowing about 'good' and 'evil.' I also knew people who were from the Catholic Church—they helped to take care of people and I wanted to do the same thing. I knew about the Catholic Church; they had fed us and brought us clothing and gave my Mama all the stuff she could rip them off for.

African Folk Religion

I asked Pee if he could take me to see a fetish priest [Some African religions use fetishes, or statuettes, to represent spiritual beings]. He said to me, "You don't want to go there." I said, "I do." I knew he needed money for school so I said, "I will give you twenty more dollars if you take me to see one." He agreed to. When I got there, there were so many people from all over Africa and from different parts of the world. They gave all of us different kinds of things to do. Everything they asked me to do I did. It came down to just a few of us left, because others had been eliminated or told they were not ready. They asked more questions and Pee would interpret for me. I was asked the same question all the other people had been asked, but they could not answer the question. The question was, "What is the color of the wall in the room and what is in the room?" I answered, "The room is red and there is a lion and some leopards, and a hippopotamus." The animals were statues made out of wood. They were large pieces with a mat and a bowl and some water on the floor. He said, "Step forward" and he put my hand up; I would be the one that was chosen for him to teach black magic. He went back into the hut and about 30 to 45 men and women came out of the hut and formed a line. He said to my interpreter, "She cannot come in here." They were angry and were shoving me, so I said to Pee: "Say to them, I will not move until someone tells me what I am doing wrong." The chief fetish priest came close to my face and said, "You are 'Jesus-baby.' If you come in here all of us will die." I was not 'Jesus-baby.' All I knew about 'Jesus' was that

He was bad. I wasn't even a believer in 'Jesus,' and I was not thinking of becoming a Christian. I just wanted to learn 'black magic' so I could help people. But those men and women formed a chain like a people's fence, walled around the big hut, and I was not getting in because they thought I was 'Jesus-baby.' I was so mad I used every curse word I could muster up, just yelling and screaming at them. The only thing I really knew about 'Jesus' was from the pastor who used to come to sleep with me at Mama's house. He had made me say the name of 'Jesus' while he was hurting me and when he was having sex with me. He would say it over and over. I really did not want anything to do with that 'Jesus.' I knew about 'God' and that He helped people.

Learning About 'Jesus'

I remember when I first became a Christian [See p. 48]. I would have bad headaches and sometimes pass out after being in church and hearing people call on the name of 'Jesus Christ.' To me He was the one hurting people, so why would these people think that I would have anything to do with that type of person? It would be two years later before I truly became a Christian that I would learn the true character of this man they call 'Jesus Christ.' It would be another twenty years before I learned that His real name was "*Yah'shua*" *HaMashiach* (the Messiah). The enemy knew who I was then because I was accusing 'Jesus' of sexually abusing me. It wasn't Him, it was a deceiving demon that dwelled in me, and I needed true deliverance. But there was no one to give me the strength to walk away from the evil he was doing to me. For hate had already built a case against my Savior. But "**Father Yah'uah**" had chosen me from the foundation of this world [See Ephesians 1:4: "…just as He chose us in Him before the foundation of the world, that we should be holy and without blame before Him in love"]. And the enemy knew that "*Yah'shua*" loved me even when I did not love Him. The enemy knew that it was a matter of time before "*Yah'shua*" would reveal His love to me. As I write this I'm remembering an incident that I had not remembered until today—that same pastor and my Mama had bitten me on my back. And Mama frequently burnt me with her cigarettes, because when he told me to say "Thank you, 'Jesus'" I would not always say it. I don't know why I would not say it; I just could not bring myself to say words of any kind. At those times I was absent from my body; I was seeing things through the eyes of a child. When he came around me I knew what the drill was but I would be off dancing in my head or I would be seeing things through the eyes of a child. Sometimes I could not feel anything that was going on or being done to me or with me. Not only could I not feel, I could not see.

One of the little girls who were at Mama's house was blind; I can't remember her name but I spent a lot of time in the fenced cage with her. We were always in the dark; it was as though I had completely disappeared. Like her I could not see what was going on or what was happening to me. It was like I was watching everyone from a distance and I was someplace else, dancing. Now that I think about it, I wanted to learn magic because somehow I believed it could help me disappear and I could help adults not to be hurt or children not to be afraid. Children do not realize that magic is really demonic. I really had not remembered why I wanted to know magic until this very second.

I thank "**Father Yah'uah**" for allowing me to write this book. It has helped me find the real missing pieces of me. There have been so many things I did not understand, especially all the confusion that surrounded my life. It's almost like I'm being unraveled from a big ball. I'm being released from many years of confinement in a prison, for as long as I can remember. I wanted to do things that would cause people not to hurt or suffer. I wanted to stop all forms of neglect and abuse that could be afflicted on others. I thought that because they did not know magic they were hurting. Because they did not have the ability to take care of them self and did not have the basic things they needed, I was thinking if only I could do magic and make Mama love me and my brothers and sisters. That's what I was thinking. As I've said, it is like I am going through a whole bunch of garbage and it stinks so badly, but I still have to sift through the garbage so I can find me.

Dressed for Church

When I started going to church it was difficult for me. The people dressed so differently; they covered up everything. I didn't understand why some of the ladies were so beautiful but they had on 'grandma dresses.' They had their heads covered up with those big ugly hats, and every time they opened their mouths they used the name of 'Jesus,' in almost every conversation. Some of them needed makeup but they did not use it. I was thinking to myself, "I do not want to look like any of them; how did their husbands or their men let them out of the house looking like that?" I probably was the only lady who dressed up to go to church. When I say 'dressed up' I mean, 'dressed improperly,' but I didn't know that these ladies wanted to look like that. I had my big earrings in my ears, my eyes dazzling in eyeliner and blue eye shadow on my eyelids that sparkle. I had deep-water red lipstick; on my lips I had bronze foundation; on my cheeks I had rosy gloss on them. I put on every drop of that makeup, but I still could not look at my face in the mirror. And if I did, I did not like what I was seeing. I could not see me; I did not think I was gorgeous to look at. My clothes were gorgeous and how my body was shaped, and I thought to myself: "Girl, you got it going on." The ladies in the church would hold on to their men friends or husbands tightly. I was thinking that they did not have to worry about me; I had several men friends and I did not want any of theirs. I just loved dressing sexy like Marilyn Monroe; she was so beautiful to me and I loved the way she dressed. In all the magazines the women looked beautiful and wore very sexy clothes, and

I wanted to look like them. One of the mothers of the church gave me some black thread and a needle. I thought to myself, "What does she want me to do with this?" I did not know how to sew. I had on a black dress with a split that went straight up to my hips. You could see almost everything when I walked, but I did not know I was naked or improperly dressed. I thought I looked like the people in the magazines. I didn't really know why the ladies chose to dress the way they did and it made me feel that I looked better than them and my clothing fit me better than theirs. You could see the outline of my whole figure; my clothing looked better than theirs did on them. I thought they were just jealous because mine looked better, and the men looked at me when I came in to the church.

I had been taught as a little girl how to dress seductively, but no one told me it was seductive. It was just said, "That looks pretty on you," but I knew the way I was built. It was true that I was ugly, but in my mind's eye the clothing made me feel good. It looked pretty on me and it made the people pay attention to me. I thought, "The ladies are jealous of me;" they were just being mean to me because I looked so good. If I sat on a bench they all would take their children and husbands and move. I thought, "Oh well, I never get invited to anything with the church members." I was just doing my own thing. As usual, doing my own thing was wrong. The church always asked me for money, but never invited me to anything that was going on at the church. I was never invited to anyone's house. And when the ladies did speak to me it was always in a mean way. One lady said to me, "Why do you dress like that? Are you trying to take somebody's husband? What example are you setting for our children and the young people here?" In all reality I didn't have a clue to what she was talking about. At that time if you said something to me that I thought was mean, then I was going to do it right back to you. Whatever came out of my mouth I just let it roll out? I had no control over what I said to anybody. If someone started a fight and I could not get away from her, then it was on, but I would give her fair warning. I looked at her without yelling. I said to her in a very soft voice, "I had two husbands and I didn't want either one of them; what makes you think I want your man, who I see crying like a little girl for no reason at all?" To me he was crying for nothing. I would not want a man who cried more than I did. What have you got yourself into? And if you let your children be children, instead of making them sit down from nine o'clock in the morning until three in the afternoon without any food, maybe you would be setting a better example for them. I said, "In fact, if you'd let those children be children, they wouldn't be as bad as they are." I said it in a soft voice, but with mean intent. I didn't smile or take my eyes off the group of ladies. I knew in my heart that if any of them had tested me, a couple of us would have been going to the hospital. At that point I was tired of them and they knew it, so they walked away saying, "She's nothing but the devil." I had heard that all my life, so hearing that from them didn't bother me one little bit.

Introduction to the Bible

One of the ladies who had been sitting nearby was shaking her head. Later on the next day she came to my house. She knocked on the door. When I answered the door she said, "Can I come in and visit with you for a while?" Everything in me knew she came to start trouble with me, so I slammed the door in her face, saying "No" as I did it. The next day she came again. I thought to myself, "I just need to go on and beat her up. That will teach the rest of them a lesson." I thought to myself that they were sending the worst one from the church to deal with me, and in reality they were. She was armed with the most deadly weapons one could have had—she had the Bible, her two children, and that smile. She was going to slay a demon and I was letting him use me to the fullest extent. My mind was not thinking on 'Godly' things; I was thinking completely like a street-person.

The next time when she came she had her two little girls with her; they were beautiful children and very quiet. She said, "I thought I would come and check on you today to make sure you were okay," then she smiled. She said, "Can my daughters please use your bathroom?" I was not thinking; I should have known it was a setup for me straight from the throne of "**Father Yah'uah**" She came every day. We talked about everything except the Bible. We talked about cooking. She let me bake cookies for her girls. I always had something special when the girls came by. I called Margaret and asked her if she would send me some clothing for the girls and baby dolls, and a tea set. I knew this mother was struggling, especially with her husband being on the road and her raising her girls without his presence. As always, whatever I needed to help someone Margaret would provide me with the money to do so. Margaret would give me that same old song and dance: "You can't, Gloria, take care of the whole world; what about you?" And as always I would convince her they needed someone to be on their side, and besides, one day it will all come back to her.

I'm going to call the children's mother 'Chanel' because I cannot remember her name. She would call me two or three times a day. We would plan things to do with the girls for the next day. One day she asked me, "Would you like to have a Bible study?" I said, "Okay." She opened up her Bible and said, "What would you like to study? What do you want to learn about?" She asked me to pick the lesson, but I did not know much about the Bible. In fact, I only knew what I had heard the pastor say plus Psalm twenty-three, which my sister 'Hot Mama' had taught me. She said, "Okay then, and let's start at the beginning." She said, "Now Genesis means the beginning." She began reading to me the names of the books of the Bible.

After this first session I could not wait for her to come back again. I had thousands of questions, some she could answer and some she could not. Every day I was up early cooking lunch, making sure my house was clean, having toys and stuff ready for the children to play with so we could start our Bible study. This went on for about two months, but one day her husband came home and so for about two weeks there were no Bible studies. She had told me her husband was coming home so she and her girls would need to spend some time with him, but I wanted to hear my next story. So I became mad and disgruntled with her. After her husband left she wanted to begin Bible study again. I said to her, "I really don't want you to come here anymore." I had hurt her feelings, and I didn't care. I felt like she had stopped me from learning, just like my Mama had done. Two days later she came; she said, "I just wanted to check on you." I said, "I'm fine" and slammed the door in her face. The very next day she came again and knocked on the door. When I opened it she had her two little girls with her. She said, "My babies have a present for you." They had a box all wrapped up in beautiful paper and with bows on it. Margaret was the only person who ever gave me any presents. Even now I always get excited when I receive something from someone. I always get so excited when I get boxes in the mail or someone gives me something wrapped up. She watched me very closely when I unwrapped the present. It was a Bible, my first Bible. It was beautiful. It was a Thomas Nelson Study Bible in black leather. I asked 'God' if he could teach me how to read all of the books in the Bible. So I began watching more and more of Sesame Street. I did not want anyone else to read for me or tell me stories from the Bible; I wanted to read for myself so I would know exactly what was in the Bible.

Reaction to the Name of 'Jesus'

'Chanel' continued to teach me and answer all of my questions that she could. When we got to the New Testament that is when the problems began, because there was the name of 'Jesus Christ.' I began to have bad seizures, my nose would bleed, and sometimes I would pass out. When I heard so many people calling on the name of 'Jesus Christ' I became so aggressive and angry with everybody.

Reaction to Ministers of 'God'

I did not want people around me because I didn't want anyone touching me. 'Chanel' wanted to come to my house. I put a quick stop to that. I put a note on my door that read like this: "I'm in my house and I do not want anyone to knock on my door because I did not invite you; if you do you take your own life in your own hands. I especially do not want Christian people to knock on my door. If you do, I will fight you." A friend of mine actually wrote the note for me. But remembering myself at that time I know I would have fought, because I would have been thinking that that person had just disrespected me and crossed over into my territory. And you just did not come into my world unless I invited you to. When I went to church I did not allow the other ladies to talk to me or touch me. I sat in the back with 'the look' on my face and I stayed quietly. I did not ask questions, and I did not give answers. I gave them dirty looks so they knew not to try and talk to me. So when they wanted me to do something they would send a man or the pastor of the church; they were afraid of me. I had not done anything bad to them, but I would not connect with anyone. They did not want me sitting by them or in the back by myself. So the man that the pastor sent to tell me to move up to the front could not wait to use his voice of authority on me, not knowing he could not command me. If he used a strong commanding voice I would rebel against him every time. When he took me by my arm I jerked away from him; I looked him straight in his eyes and said to him, "If you touch me again I'll kill you." He backed away from me. After the service, the pastor and some of the ladies of the church and some of the men came to talk to me. They were talking but I could not hear them. They were still talking when I went out the door. I don't know why I felt like they were all going to do something to me; I think it was because I had been trying to understand who 'Jesus' was. But I had not grasped it yet, and I was afraid of Him. Somehow I thought something bad was going to happen to me if I let 'Jesus Christ' into my life. I thought that if I kept his people out I would be able to keep Him out. I did not understand why they all loved 'Jesus,' but I did not. I needed to know why they loved Him. My brothers and sisters and I had suffered so many terrible things through people who believed or acted in His name; how could I love Him?

Drawn to 'Christ'

By this time Margaret had come home. She and my son started attending church with me. Margaret knew very little about 'Jesus' and 'God,' but the whole family was trying. I knew my life could not go on the way it had, not even one more day; plus, I wanted to learn about 'Jesus.' 'Chanel' had read much of the Old Testament to me, but I did not want to know what was in the New Testament because I did not want to be involved with 'Jesus Christ.' Yet I was compelled to read the Bible. And If I did, I could have my final revenge on the people who loved 'Jesus.' I could show them how evil and unloving He was; yes, that was my intent. But I could not read a lot of big words. Words like 'look' and 'see,' 'him' and 'her,' 'cat' and 'dog' were the limit of my ability and understanding at that particular time. Those were the only words I could read, so I asked 'God' if He would teach me more words. I had a new mission now and a goal. I was going to prove once and for all that all this mumbo-jumbo about loving 'Jesus Christ' was wrong. I began to read something every day, and I was not afraid to ask people what a word meant. I was learning and I understood almost everything. Sometimes I would have to read one story over and over again before I could begin to understand it. Sometimes it would not make sense to me at first, but I kept reading the same story over and over again and then something would happen – I would understand!

I remember one time Darrell McGee said to me, "I don't know if you are really intelligent and trying to fool the rest of us, because you know this Bible so well. You show me things in it that I may not have seen." When I started reading the Bible stories Darrell said, "Gloria, you make me think about the stories I read." Darrell and Yvonne McGee's daughter, Lonnie, now considers me as her grandmother. Darrell says I am one of the most intelligent persons he knows when it comes to understanding the Bible. Darrell and Yvonne always encourage me in the love of 'Jesus Christ.' Not only was I a part of the family of 'Jesus', but he said I was a part of theirs. They always made me feel good about my understanding of the things I would put my hand to, even when I decided that at age 53 I wanted to take *'tae kwon do.'* Darrell said, "If you believe you're not too old, go for it, Gloria." Without my realizing it I was falling in love with 'Jesus Christ.' When I read about how they crucified him, how He asked His father to forgive them, it touched my heart; I would be reading and crying at the same time. How could He love them? I was trying to understand why he didn't call the Angels and handle his business. Instead he decided to forgive them. They even tried to kill him when he was a baby the people who should have loved Yahshua the Messiah and been happy that He was in the world wanted to see him dead. It was the people that he came into this world to save, including me, who wanted him dead. They did not understand the love of 'God' ("**Father Yah'uah**" *Elohim*) for them. They were just as stupid as I was to think 'Jesus Christ' was the one who was doing them wrong. He made a willing choice to give up His rights so that we could live without our sins he forgiven us. We should make that same choice to give up our lives for Him. Some of us will make it, some of us won't or can't. The man I had once hated I now loved. I still wanted to learn more about

'Jesus Christ;' there was no turning back now. Even when I tried to go back into the world I could not. I just didn't fit in so I prayed and asked the 'Lord' 'God' (*Adonai* "**Yah'uah**"), "Please forgive me. And help me to make the change. I do not know how to change me and to stop me from doing all the evil things and thoughts that I have, but I believe with my whole heart that your only-begotten Son 'Jesus Christ' died on the 'cross' [stake] for the sins of the entire world. Please 'Jesus,' I pray that I will stop hating the people of 'God;' and please help me not be mad all the time. Teach me to love you, 'Jesus' ("*Yah'shua*"); teach me who you really are."

Jesus the Messiah and the 'Holy Spirit'

I had been a Christian for about six or seven years now. I had accepted 'Jesus' the 'Christ' into my life but I still did not know how to give my all to Him. I wanted to tell Him all the things I had done but I thought if He knew everything, He wouldn't love me anymore. I could not risk losing 'Jesus' (*"Yah'shua"*) the Messiah.

I started going to another church. This church was a mixed congregation, rich and poor, undertaking work together for the glory of 'Jesus' (*"Yah'shua"*) the Messiah. It was called Hinesville Christian Fellowship. The people were really 'off the chain.' They were helping others to grow, and I was able to hear the message for the first time. The preacher wasn't screaming. He wasn't jumping all over the place. He was merely talking. I could feel my heart bursting wide open. I could not wait for the days to pass to go to church again. I wanted so much to be there. I would go home and read all night, and for the next four years I was hooked. There was no drinking, there was no going to clubs and there was not even dancing in my head. There wasn't any more confusion in my mind's eye.

Yet I had not encountered the 'Holy Spirit.' I knew about **"Father Yah'uah."** I knew about *"Yah'shua the Messiah."* I had heard about the 'Holy Spirit' but had no connection with Him. Everything I needed I would ask 'God' ("**Father Yah'uah**" *Elohim*) for, but I never talked to the 'Holy Spirit.' The 'Holy Spirit' was whispering to me love and compassion. I was saying, "I love you too, but I only need 'God' ("**Father Yah'uah**" *Elohim*)." I could not share the darkest 'monster' that still dwelled inside me. In I thought the Holy Spirit would tell on me because he knows all truth. When my pastor left the church, I would not go again because I did not want to accept the new pastor and his family. I wanted Dicky and Brenda Welch back. I wanted my pastor and his wife to come back to us, with all my faults bad temper and being as mean as a snake. They love me and I was able to love them back. But that was not going to happen. They left the goats and sheep's. I was so angry I didn't want anyone or anything to enter my life. I knew I was able to keep quiet for a while the monster which still lived inside of me, but now it was ready to blow up and take it out on anyone and everything. In the meantime I was running 'The Heart of Christ, Inc.'. I was feeding and clothing people. I was also praying with people. I was visiting the sick. I was cleaning and cooking for people. Miss Deborah would take me to Florida to minister to people through Bible studies and by preaching in churches. Outside of Hinesville I had helped start churches with people whom nobody wanted in their church. I would minister to them, help them to get back in the church and help them get off drugs. I'd help pastors get back in the word of 'God' ("**Father Yah'uah**" *Elohim*). But I still was messed up inside, from sunup to sundown. I had to continuously be doing something so no one could know how messed up I was. I was always concerned about the things people said about me. It would take me out of my peace with "**Father Yah'uah**." Sometimes I would shut down for a whole year. The only people I would associate with were the unsaved sinners. I would bring them into a place where they were willing to accept 'Jesus' ("*Yah'shua*") the Messiah as being given to them by 'God' ("**Father Yah'uah**" *Elohim*) to be the Savior of this world when they had confessed Him as their Savior, I would back out of their lives, not wanting any real attachments to them.

I met a chaplain at Fort Stewart. I'm going to call him 'Derek.' We dated for a while. Then he wanted to have sex with me. I refused. I had told him some things about myself, and I wanted someone who loved "**Father Yah'uah**" our *Elohim* enough that he would not sin with me. He was browbeating me during our whole relationship. When I visit him I was out of his house by 6:30 pm, no later than seven o'clock. We once went to a movie. There was a lot of cursing and men and women having sex with the same sex. I said to him, "I do not want to see this movie." He said, "I paid for it already." So I got up and left the movie. He was so upset about it. I don't think that he expected me to leave the movie. He had not expected me to say "No!" to things that I thought were not glorifying 'God' (" **Father Yah'uah**" *Elohim*). The things you let into your spirit man that are not of "**Father Yah'uah**" *Elohim* are surely the things that will destroy you. I said "no" to sexual intercourse with him. So I lost the man, but I gained something. I gained a stronger relationship with my Father and my Savior. I was not going to allow my body to be manipulated or used in any improper way, not to get a husband or anything else. I had already done those sorts of things and they had not turned out good for me. It was hard and painful for me, but at that moment **"Father Yah'uah"** delivered me from another fear, the fear of me being a sex slave. For a man so he could become my husband in take care of me. I knew that. Was the job of Father Yah'uah and Yahshua the Messiah, and the Holy Spirit? It was their job to take care of me. I knew I didn't have to do what others wanted me to do to please them. I knew I had a purpose in the kingdom of 'God' (**"Father Yah'uah"** *Elohim*) and *"Yah'shua"* His Son. I looked at all the things **"Father Yah'uah"** had brought me out of. So many times he had delivered me, even from my own self. How could He not be real?

Life in Hinesville

During this time I was homeless. I was working every single day from five in the morning sometimes to one o'clock at night or later. A restaurant owner, Mr. Poole, allowed me to use his bathroom at Poole's Deli to wash up and he made sure I did not go hungry. He would allow me to pay for my food from him whenever I got the money. If I could not pay he never bothered me about me paying. He also provided food for my clients at no charge. Mr. Poole and his wife and daughter were real good to me and the people I was serving.

At that time I was sleeping in my car. When I lost my car, I was sleeping at 'The Heart of Christ, Inc.' or in the cemetery. I did not miss one day of work. When I got sick and had to go in the hospital, I conducted business from my hospital bed. I know what you're thinking: "In the cemetery?" Being from New York City, I knew if you were homeless that the safest place for you to be. My brother Sonny had made that clear to me that the cemetery was the safest place to be. Because no one will bother you there—they're too afraid! I also slept on people's floors. Although every pastor in town knew I was homeless, only one pastor allowed me to stay two months with her. That was Pastor Dacey Edwards. Her husband and her was my first pastor's. I stayed with one of her church members too for a short time; her name was Niece Johnson. I was helping people, putting them in hotels, helping them get apartments, and making sure they had food to eat and clean clothes on their back, and shoes on their feet yet I didn't have a place to live myself. I was donating trailers and cars, trucks even a boat; whatever was given to me I would give to the people in need. I was not getting paid except for one year. Everybody was so upset when I did get paid; I would put the money into the heart of Christ that people had given me for myself and from my SSI. Check then I would pay myself and then I would take the money and put it right back into the ministry. To ensure that the ministry had money I would even put into 'The Heart of Christ, Inc.' my monthly check from SSI [Supplemental Security Income, a program of the Federal Government to help the disabled]. In my mind I was thinking that whatever it took, I would give whatever came in to people who were in need so no parent would have to mistreat their children as we were mistreated. That's what kept me going. I knew my mama had abused us because of things she wanted and money, so money has no real value to me. I only need it so I can buy what I have to.

Interaction with Other Organizations and the City

I resigned from the United Way because one of the ladies that worked for them said I could not help the Mexican people because most of them were illegal. So I thought to myself, "I have to give them their money back if I help the Mexican people." Once again my heart was troubled. How could I deny any person food and clothing? When a person is hungry and without clothing they have already been dehumanized; their stomachs do not know they are a certain nationality. Hunger is worldwide and it produces the same effects: pain, sorrow, and horror. It turns people into liars and thieves. I know; I lived it. I called a friend and asked her to write a letter for me. It was my resignation from United Way. I was not trying to be arrogant or stubborn or mean. I knew what it was to be hungry, and hunger has no respecter of persons. How could I deny any parent the opportunity to give their children those things that were needed for life? I made a hard choice. It was said to me, "You're biting off the hands that is actually feeding you." I replied no Father Yah'uah was actually feeding me. I fell out of favor with the Christian family and with some of the city officials of Hinesville, Georgia. They were to help me grow, and although they did not know it, they were helping me to be a better person by some of the harsh things they did to me. So I'm grateful—not cynical, not prideful, but grateful to them for that. I do not regret the decision I made. I only regret not having the support I needed from people who had the proper education to run the office and business side of the ministry. Those things I did not know how to do, but I did know how to treat people with respect and to help them see their self-worth. Because Christians people of Hinesville help me see myself as a human being. I wanted to obtain a grant so I paid a man $3000 to put a grant together for me. I needed the city to partner with me. At that time there were only pastors on my board. One of the men said, "I'll take it to the city to ask them to partner with you." The city officials said to me, "You don't have statistics." I replied, "I did files on everyone and I have social security numbers and addresses." They asked me to give them all of the files so they could compile the paperwork, so I did. The city received the grant but had cut me completely out of it, claiming that one of the city officials had found the grant and put this grant together. Well, he did not all he did was call all of the city agencies together. Now I was out of $3000 and no agency would work with me and no lawyer would help me challenge the city officials of Hinesville. The government agency that I applied for the paperwork for the grant from said, "Cities do this to small agencies all the time; there is nothing we can do to help you." The pastors on my board who could've helped did nothing. It was said to me, "You're just like a postman. You just delivered the package to the city." Now my agency was an outcast by the pastors in the city. One of the pastors said to me, "Why are you crying about this?" I remember his exact words: He said, "It is like you are talking to different people and each of them is asking me the same question; when I answer you start crying all over again and again like you are hearing it for the first time." Was I? They gathered by the back door and began to talk among themselves as I went to the bathroom to wash my face. I was wondering, "Why did he say that?" They did not see me when I came from the bathroom. I overheard one of them say, "We all need to withdraw our support from her and force her to close down." But I heard Pastor Herman Scott say "I heard 'God' say, 'Help Gloria.'"

I can remember that day as though it happened today. The feeling that I felt was that 'Jesus' (*"Yah'shua"*) loved me. All of my life I had never felt like I was a real person. I never felt like I belonged to anybody. And I knew that there was no one other than my children and daughter-in-law and Kincade Douglas who loved me. But that day Pastor Herman Scott brought me into a place with 'Jesus' (*"Yah'shua"*) and 'God' (**"Father Yah'uah"** *Elohim*) that I will never forget. It was like all the broken pieces inside of me were finally being put together as one. I was being made whole. The scattered pieces of my life were being drawn together. Pastor Scott was not seeing me with his human eyes. He was seeing me with Father Yah'uah's love while the others were only looking at my flesh. He is the only pastor that was on my board that was not on it for his own glory and certainly not for the contributions he made to the organization he really wanted to see people being made whole and I was one of them.

Back to School

I was 53 years old. I still did not have a high school diploma. My bookkeeper, Ms. Dorothy Woods, taught me how to count money. Also the head teller at First Citizens Bank, Ms. Brenda, is one of the most humble people I have ever met. She always makes me feel real important. She's never told me whether she was a Christian or not, but you can sense the 'Holy Spirit' always radiating out of her. I really love all the people at that bank. If I would miscount the money, she would make the corrections and explain to me what she was doing. If I didn't get it the first time, she would take her time until she was sure I understood. That is a very good quality for any banker. Mr. Roberts and Lydia Clark also helped me learn how to count by using cards. They would always tell me things to make me laugh so I wouldn't be nervous. I really miss them since I moved so far away. At times when it was too cold to be outside, I stayed in their home with them.

Col. Roy Tunnage, Mrs. Deborah Tunnage, Mr. Roy's mother Ms. Yvonne Tunnage, the Tunnages' daughters, Debran, Charlie and Devin, and Maj. Ronald Ellyson and family helped prepare me to get my GED. Vocational Rehabilitation in Hinesville, Georgia paid for me to take some college courses on how to use a computer. I had never walked through a college building. It was the happiest day of my life. You cannot believe the joy I had going on inside of me before I took those college courses. I bought a computer, and I would have friends come and teach me how to use it. By the time I started taking college courses, I had about 15 used computers. I was determined to learn all I could about computers in my class. No one knew anything about computers except me and my teacher. But he did not know I knew anything. One day he was late, stuck in traffic. The phone kept ringing and no one would answer it. I got up from my seat, picked up the phone and I said, "Good morning. This is Armstrong Atlantic State University Continuing Education. I am Gloria Christ, can I help you please?" For a few moments there was silence. It was my teacher. Then he asked me how much I knew about computers. I said I'd taken apart a whole lot of them and put them back together again. He asked me to teach the class, so I said, "I can teach the class." Then I taught the class until he got there. He sat down and watched me. He said thank you. And then he asked me, "What are you doing here?"

On October 26, 1999 I completed 20 hours of class and I got my certificate from Robinson College of Business for the introduction to computers class. And on May 10, 2000 I received a certificate from Armstrong Atlantic State University. Next I received my high school diploma from Cornerstone Christian Correspondence School. Then on December 30, 2002 I received my Associate of Religious Arts degree in Biblical Studies. On May 25, 2003 I received my ordination certificate. In 2004 I received my license as Rev. Gloria Wynter Christ. The action of my city caused change in my life rather good or bad, cause me to take a long look at my limited knowledge. Their actions brought something good out of me was Father Yah'uah in all of them yes he was. What they did was the best thing for the people no matter who administered the grant, and it made me take a look at myself. And Pastor Herman Scott reached down within my soul and began pulling me out of the 'belly of hell.' He was pulling me back towards 'Jesus' (*"Yah'shua"*) and 'God' (**"Father Yah'uah"** *Elohim*). I was so concerned about taking care of people that I forgot about me; I could not see myself as a real person pastor Scott help me see me. I needs to meat who I was supposed to be. It was long overdue. So **"Father Yah'uah"** *Elohim* began guiding me to the place where He could educate me through other people. The Word of **"Father Yah'uah"** says, "For I know the plans I have for you ... plans to prosper you and not to harm you" (Jeremiah 29: 11). I couldn't see that then, but I do see it now. Some things I was ready for and some things I only thought I was ready for. The things that I thought I was ready for were all about flesh and not about **"Father Yah'uah"** *Elohim*. The actions of the people He entrusted me with caused me to cry out to **"Father Yah'uah."** He orchestrated every single act that the city officials did so he could educate me. I am still slow at some things, but it's getting better. In their decision was the best thing for the people.

The Word of 'God' (**"Father Yah'uah"** *Elohim*) began to teach me to seek and trust only the Spirit of **"Father Yah'uah,"** that is, the 'Holy Spirit.' I had so much I wanted to learn and very few people to teach me. I did not know in reality the people were teaching me. And the world kept pointing me to the 'Holy Spirit' and He began to teach me, because every person I needed to teach me something was there. And

I began to feel something I had never felt before, except with my children; I began to feel that I could love people back. I wasn't fighting within my soul anymore. The word of "**Father Yah'uah**" became so sweet to my ears. I would have questions and His 'Holy Spirit' would give me answers. Not only did He give me answers, He showed me where they were in the books of the Bible. How could this be? I couldn't touch Him. I couldn't see Him, but He must be real for I could feel Him in the people and in the answers He gave me from his Word. It became easier and easier for me to read and learn from His Word. Yes, Father Yah'uah was in every last person that entered into my life rather they were good or bad, Father Yah'uah used them to bring deliverance to me.

The 'Holy Spirit' began to reveal things to me through reading the Word of 'God' ("**Father Yah'uah**" *Elohim*). Because of that, I got in trouble. I was taking a leadership class in one of the local churches where I knew the pastor had a heart for Father Yah'uah at that time he was my pastor. Before that he volunteered for the heart of Christ he was the pastor of one of the largest congregation before he was a pastor he had worked with me. He was a very tall man, built like a lumberjack. He had so much love for people, his compassion, and his ability to show mercy was unusual for me to see in one person. The class was given a scripture assignment by the teachers. I chose the topic of Adam and Eve. While studying I found out that "**Father Yah'uah**" *Elohim* never cursed Adam and Eve. He cursed the serpent and the ground because of Adam. To Eve He said, "I will greatly multiply your sorrow in childbearing (pregnancy); in pain you shall bear children" (Genesis 3: 16). When you think about it and listen to what the words are saying to you, you will see that Eve was going to have some type of pain, but not severe. "Greatly multiply your sorrow" were the words that the 'Holy Spirit' made stand! Out to me. In order to multiply something you have to already have something. So I shared what I understood about this with the class. Then I was asked to change the paper and admit that 'God' (**"Father Yah'uah"** *Elohim*) had indeed pronounced a curse on Adam and Eve. However the first man that the Bible records that **"Father Yah'uah"** directly pronounced a curse on was Cain for murdering Abel. There were 15 people in that room. They all got a chance to yell and scream at me and tell me how disrespectful I was of the pastor. I wasn't trying to be disrespectful of him, not at all. I respected him very much as a man of 'God' ("Father **Yah'uah**" *Elohim*), but I loved **"Father Yah'uah"** too much to deny what His 'Holy Spirit' had shown me. And I would not back down from the true

I was in a 'Catch-22' situation. If I said that the class was right, then I was saying that the Bible was wrong; but the class wouldn't let me say that they were wrong. So I let them finish fussing with me. Then the pastor said, "You need to pray about what church you should be in because this is not it." Then he said, "All you have to do is say what I'm telling you to say." I kept my eyes cast down to the floor to show my respect for him. Then he said to me, "You cannot attend any more of the leadership class." I begged him in front of all those people; I begged him not to take the class from me that day. I said, "Please don't take this from me. Please don't stop me from studying." And he replied, "Why can't you just say it?" I raised my eyes up and said, "I'm from New York City, and I grew up in Fort Greene, Brooklyn. I know what games are, and this is a game. And you are the leader." It may sound like I was being disrespectful, but I wasn't. I was telling the truth and sometimes the truth is not what people want to hear. I stayed in church for a month after that I stopped going to church. I believe the pastor and the other man studied the Scriptures and found out for them-selves. I was telling the truth. They came to my shop about a week later and said I could come back to church. They said it was the way that I gave the presentation that upset everyone. They totally forgot that all I did was refuse to accept their answer over **"Father Yah'uah"** *Elohim*'s word. I still believe that the pastor of that congregation is one of the best pastors I have ever met. What I learned from that experience is that **"Father Yah'uah"** has given us a true teacher, His very own Spirit. He will lead you into all truth.

Lots of times people will come to me and say, "Can we do a Bible study?" With me and I say, "Yes." Then they go preach their sermon and say, "The 'Holy Spirit' showed me this." I used to get mad because they would say, "The 'Holy Spirit' taught me this," and I thought it was not the 'Holy Spirit.' But me **"Father Yah'uah"** had to teach me that whatever I learned was not just for me. It was for the people of His kingdom and those who had a strong desire to know Him. He communicates with us, so the person wasn't lying. The 'Holy Spirit' that communicates with me was teaching them through me. **"Father Yah'uah"** showed me the pride and bigotry attitude that can be in me. *"Yah'shua"* prayed "...that they all may be one, as You, Father, are in Me, and I in You; that they also may be one in Us, that the world may believe that You sent Me" (John 17:21). He also said, "I can of myself do nothing...I do not seek my own will but the will of the Father who sent me" (John 5:30). That is how we should live every day. Where do we see and hear what we should do? We see and hear it in the Bible and in our hearts and we know when the Word is right. But we have to understand that the Holy Spirit, Yahshua the Messiah and **"Father Yah'uah"** works in his people to points us back to Father, **"Yah'uah"** Himself, and to His only-begotten Son, *"Yah'shua"* the Messiah.

The most important thing that I got out of the study of Adam and Eve was the mercy and love that **"Father Yah'uah"** *Elohim* had for them, even though they had sinned against Him. If you look real closely all the way back to the beginning, you will see the tenderness of **"Father Yah'uah"** *Elohim*, even to Cain. He also showed that tenderness to me and to you today! Love is always an action and motion, and **"Father Yah'uah"** always shows it. I have the 'right' to hate those who hate me and who desire to see me destroyed. But the word of **"Father Yah'uah"** says, "Love your enemies…and pray for those who spitefully use you" (Matt. 5:44). This I finally understand and now know what it really means.

The People of Hinesville

"**Father Yah'uah**" has used the people of Hinesville, Georgia to help me and many others from all over the United States and other countries. He has used me for that purpose, also and in the process He was healing me through the people that his 'Holy Spirit' had assigned to me.

Geneva Pitt was one of them. She was a 'baby Christian,' and she just wanted to be in the presence of 'God.' One of the most intelligent young ladies I had met, and she was hungry for "*Yah'shua*" who was real to her. She always wanted us to study. She wanted every single question answered about the Father ("**Yah'uah**") and His 'Holy Spirit,' as well as "*Yah'shua*," His only-begotten Son. She wanted it all, no matter what she saw me do. She always held me in the greatest respect. One of the questions she asked me was, "Gloria, why do you allow people to treat you like they do? And you continue to be their friend?" I said, "Trust me." I did not like the way people treated me. I had to learn to love them. I had to learn that they had to come first. I had to learn that I couldn't hurt them, so I got quiet and stayed away from them. I believed that whenever they were ready to be friends again, they would say so. I had been homeless, but now Geneva let me stay in her house. For almost three years, even when she went overseas, she let me stay there. When she moved, she let me move into her new house. She trusted in me and always believed that I was a good person, though sometimes I simply was not a good person in front of her. She helped me to become a good person, because of the love she showed me. Her desire for me was to see me continue in the word of 'God' ("Father **Yah'uah**" *Elohim*). She made me want to study. She had so many questions, and I wanted to know the answers too. So I had to study so I could give her the right answers.

At that same time I met Jessica at church. When most of the women rejected me, Ms. Jessica was the only one that accepted me without expecting me to change the way I saw Messiah "*Yah'shua*" She and her husband had a way of ministering to people that brought much truth. I watched how the people of "*Yah'shua*" the Messiah would say how much they loved Him and her and how they did so many good works in the church. Jessica has a 'voice like an angel,' but at times they would deny her the right to sing. I watched her go through all kinds of tribulations with them and stay at peace with 'Jesus' ("*Yah'shua*") even though she knew they were hurting her. I used to ask, "**Father Yah'uah**," please show me how Jessica can do it." One day while praying for her family, the 'Holy Spirit' said to me, "Because she loves 'Jesus' ("*Yah'shua*") she does it with the Father's love inside of her. She has the right to fight, but she chooses to love through the bumps and bruises. She gets up and goes straight to the Father's throne, Gloria that is how she does it." It was something for me to think about. Will I learn to ever do that?

I had known Col. Brenda Mason for about six months when I obtained my Associate in Religious Arts degree, and I wanted to attend the Jacksonville Theological Seminary to get my B.A. in religious social work. The cost of it was $2,500, but I was homeless at the time. Another friend of mine, who was a professor once at a university, asked me to let her keep my books and tapes at her house. She would study them and then be able to help me the best she could. I agreed. She moved but never returned my tapes; besides that I needed someone to write my paper in proper order for me. But I would be the one giving all of my own answers so my sister, in the name of 'Jesus,' said she would do it for a price. I paid her $300 to do that part for me, but she left. When she came back she said to me that I owed her $150 more if she was to complete the project. She moved the next day. I asked her when she came back, "Why you didn't come back?" She gave me the story that she was still putting my paperwork together and she needed the balance of the money. So I paid it to her, but she never gave me the paperwork or my books. We had a mutual friend who said the reason she would not return my books was because I needed to pay her for helping me study, but she never helped me with anything. I did everything except write my own paper. I put it on tape for her to type it up for me. I gave her all the answers to each question; I just wanted it on the paper written correctly. So I paid her $400, thinking I would get my books and tapes back, but that never happened. I've been to her home more than 10 times and still was not able to obtain my books and tapes. I already did not trust Christians. This situation made it worse because I could not understand the purpose of what she was doing. I called the school and explained to them the situation and asked if I could purchase the tapes separately. I was told I would have to pay for the course all over again. Again I could not understand why I would have to pay for the entire course when all I needed were the tapes and books. However Col. Mason gave me $2500 which allowed me to purchase the tapes and books. I finished the courses but because I was homeless my certificate was packed away. So I had to pay an additional $175 to get my ordination license, because they were not sure I took the courses. I explained to the lady my entire situation but there was no mercy or grace. That made my view of the working of my fellow brothers and sisters look even worse. Yes, they still were my brothers and sisters and I had to learn to love them in spite of what was going on in my life, I did not trust anyone who said they were a Christian until I met Mr. Roger Rice, Sr. and his wife, Sheila Rice.

My computer broke down and I had to take it to a computer repair shop. As I was driving to a client's house one day, I saw a sign that said, 'In-Home Computers.' How was I to know that this man would open my eyes to more truth? I'm going to give you a description of Mr. Roger Rice. He is very tall and a slender young man. When you watch him work, you see he loves what he does. At that moment I was about to get the lesson of my life. I waited patiently for him to finish what he was doing. He took my computer and he ran some tests. He said, "You will have to leave it with me." I thought about it for a moment; then I said, "Can you please give me a piece of paper and a pen?" He looked at me and gave them to me. My computer was open. I started to write everything down that had a serial number visible. He looked at me and tilted his head slightly and said, "Miss Christ, what are you doing?" I said, "I'm taking down all the serial numbers, so if you steal anything I will know it." Then I said, "So many of you people say that you are good people and that you are good Christians, but you are liars and thieves." He looked at me. He walked behind the counter and he got a box out. It had checks that had been written to his computer company. All of the checks were bad ones. They were from people all over our community, a whole month's worth of bad checks. All of his hard work had been paid in bad checks. Tears streaming down his face he said, "Ms. Christ, I know you are a Christian. You cannot go around hating everybody and being angry for what other people have done to you. You have to learn to trust someone." I thought, "I don't think so." In the middle of his shop with people coming in, he took the time to say, "Let's pray." He first asked 'God' to forgive all the Christian people who had hurt me. He apologized for those who had used me; he apologized on their behalf for their behavior. Tears started streaming down my face, because of the honesty of his words to 'Father Yah'uah.' Someone had said to me, "I'm sorry for what other people have done to you. Can you forgive our brothers and sisters in the name of 'Jesus'?' I could hear the Spirit of "Father **Yah'uah**" inside of me saying, "Forgive them, they're growing just like you." I thought, "Where are these feelings coming from? How could I forgive them—they were the ones who had offended me?" But my heart kept saying that 'Jesus' died on the 'cross' [stake] so that we could understand how to forgive one another. That was one of the most valuable lessons I had learned. I learned to forgive. Fifty tons felt lifted off of me that day. I could feel the change that went through me. I could sense my heart shouting, "Glory to "Father **Yah'uah**" our *Elohim*, glory to His Holy Name. *Hal'lu***YAH**! *Hal'lu***YAH**! Blessings and praise be to "Father **Yah'uah**" our *Elohim*, for His Kingdom reigns in all of His people. He lives!"

I learned that day that even the strongest Christian may do some things that are out of character. You see, we go to school to learn how to do things the right way, because most of our lives we've learned the easy way. Dying to oneself is a hard process, but we must do it every day so that the 'Holy Spirit' of "Father **Yah'uah**" can be in our hearts. Much love began to flow through me that day. This man who was going to check out my computer did more than fix my computer. He began planting seeds in me of love for my brothers and sisters in "Father Yah'shua," and so my heart began to be healed. "Father **Yah'uah**" *Elohim* had used him that day for me. I know in my heart that the 'Holy Spirit' caused me to go to him in the first place. His wife, Sheila, began helping me at 'The Heart of Christ, Inc.' by donating clothing, food, and personal items for my clients and me. In order for me to write this book, they've had to fix my computers and buy a certain type of printer for me. Ever since I've known them, they have helped me with parents who could not afford to buy computers for their children.

This is what one woman and her husband said to me about their children: "My husband has been out of work for some time. My son had to stop going to school so he could help me. We do not receive public assistance. My son and I paid all the bills because my husband can't work now. He was hurt on the job. We are Christians. I thank 'God' for my son because he helps us a lot. He's sacrificing for his three younger brothers to help me pay the bills. I could not afford to buy a computer for my children even with my son helping me. By giving us this computer my oldest son can study to get his GED and take college courses. I don't know where the money will come from to get the Internet but we will try to get a telephone. Thank you, Pastor Gloria. You and the computer man will always be in our prayers." Her husband said, "I feel like I am their father and a man again. This man who does not know me has made me feel like a real father because he has helped my son see what real Christian men do to help each other. Thank you for the Spanish Bible and the computer. Please, Pastor Gloria, say this to him for me."

Mr. and Mrs. Rice have this effect on everyone who walks into their 'In-Home Computers' business. Mr. Rice also mentors young men of all nationalities on how to become better men in the community. He takes the time to minister to them on how to start a business and how to stop stealing and living rowdy lives. He shows them what jail takes from them. He tells them if all you can do is pick up paper, then get paid for it. Be the best at whatever talent you have. He talks to them about saving and investing. He lets them know it can be done no matter how young or how old they are.

"**Father Yah'uah**" was constantly showing me Himself in people. Like Clay Sikes and his entire family have allowed me at different times to represent them in caring for the people in our community. When they could get away from their businesses they actually came and participated in helping people. Mr. and Mrs. Sikes has ministered to me many times and prayed with me. The things I have seen Attorney Robert Pirkle do for people in our community are amazing to me. He helped me incorporate 'The Heart of Christ, Inc.' as a non-profit organization.

I had to go to court once over a security system that was broken. It caused the police officers to come about 10 times. So I got fined for it. I hadn't done anything wrong except have a system put in that was faulty. On several occasions I had called the company who put the system in, but they had not come. I had even called them while the police were there and the system went off, so they knew I was telling the truth. I talked to the lady in charge at the fire station where I was fined $400. The lady said I had never talked to her. I was steaming. I said to the judge, "She is lying. I have come and spoken with her on several occasions." I was so upset that I was trembling, trying to tell the judge that I had not done anything wrong. He said, "Ms. Christ, you are the head of that organization. Someone has to take responsibility for the system going off." I said to him, "No. I am not going to pay that bill. I will go to jail first." He said to me, "Ms. Christ, why are you trying to be a martyr?" I said I was not trying to be a martyr. I just wanted justice. At that time I did not know he was giving me justice. He had the officers take me out of the courtroom and talk to me in the back. The officers told me I had a certain time to pay the money. I went to my pastor and told him I was going to jail and would he take the keys for 'The Heart of Christ, Inc.' for me? Pastor Dicky Welch went and paid the fine for me. Then he went through the tedious process of explaining to me that the judge did have mercy on me. All I could see was someone in authority trying to force me to do something that I said "no" to. Sometimes people see that you have issues, but they try to look beyond those issues because they see a bigger picture. Until I started writing this book, I didn't see the mercy that the judge had for me. He could've put me in jail not only for refusing to pay the fine, but also for being disrespectful in the courtroom I use the word disrespectful because I did not know any other word to use, but I was not trying to be disrespectful I was only trying to state facts. But the love of **"Father Yah'uah"** was in him. He saw past my hurts, past my not understanding, and he showed me more mercy than I deserved to have. The Spirit of **"Father Yah'uah"** was there working through the judge. Now I do understand what a community is. It is people working together to make each other's lives better, regardless of race or status. It is helping one another to become whole in every area of their lives. I am still learning; I am still beginning to-feeling the emotions that people are supposed to have. I know that **"Father Yah'uah"** our *Elohim* is building His kingdom inside of me. I am still a little slower than my peers, but I'm getting there; I am taking 'baby steps,' but I am slowly getting there.

My Story Continues

It's been so long since I've written anything, but whenever I try to write I don't really want to, I will get so emotionally upset about the whole thing. It is like going back into a dark closet and pulling out things that I really don't want to put my hand on. But as I said earlier, this story has to be told so that there will be peace within my soul and also that there will be no more secrets. And just maybe someone else will become whole. There will be nothing hidden for Satan to build on, for all my secrets will be out in the open, pulled up by their very roots. All their possibilities to destroy me have been overcome by the blood of "*Yah'shua*" my Messiah ('Jesus' the 'Christ'). After four months I'm writing again, and throughout this whole time I have not taken a drink or gone dancing. For that I'm so thankful to "Father **Yah'uah**" *Elohim*. But at times I begin to see things through the eyes of a child again, especially when I stumble back into those old dark places, writing down and thinking about all of the 'secrets' that Satan wants to keep hidden within my memory. I have to keep repeating to myself, "No weapon formed against me shall prosper" (Isaiah 54:17). "*Yah'shua*" the Messiah has cleansed me by His blood that He shed on Calvary for me.

After people come to faith in "*Yah'shua*" the Messiah, some of them go on to live their new Christian lives full of discouragement, hurt, confusion, rejection, dishonesty, anger, and even hatred. They can become judgmental of themselves and others. Satan's agents constantly try to beat them down as a result of the abuse that they had endured in their lives, and because they are always trying to keep their sins secret. The worst part of it is that they think that if anyone knew their secrets then they would get treated badly in blame for what went on in their lives. Most of the time people do blame the adults for what went on in their lives as children, for what they went through in their bodies and in their minds. The person themselves begins to thinking it would be used against them, that they would be looked down upon, even hated most of the time they are. The most hurtful of all is the rejection they often receive from Christian people themselves, the ones who should be helping to bring about healing. I was lucky; no, lucky is not the right word, I was blessed to have loving Christians who outweighed the judgment of those Christians who hated me because of my past. I know now that they had not grown enough in "**Father Yah'uah**." Love, they were seeking to destroy me, but there were so many who would continuously plead the blood of "*Yah'shua*" the Messiah over my life. They were not afraid of any principalities or powers that they thought may have controlled me. They knew that the blood of "*Yah'shua*" the Messiah had all power and that I had indeed been saved by His precious blood. They did not believe I was Satan's daughter.

The Name of 'God'

As I said earlier, I have always seen and heard things that other people did not perceive. I began to see and hear words that had no meaning to me. At that time I did not know that the actual Name of 'God' (*Elohim*) was "**Yah'uah.**" One day I kept hearing the sound "**Yahu**" in my mind (and I did not know then that there was a website named 'Yahoo'). When I told someone that I kept hearing the word "**Yahu**" they told me about the website; but every time I heard the word "**Yahu**" it was connected with an experience of 'God' (*Elohim*). I thought that I had really 'gone off the deep end.' There's no way that the name of 'God' could be "**Yahu**" because I knew that His name was 'God!' I kept hearing these words: "I am "**Yahu**" your 'God;' name my ministry after my Name and I will heal you and those that come to me by my Name." That was the beginning of my knowing "**Father Yah'uah**" our *Elohim* by name. But for two years I didn't understand what I was hearing. My friend Sadie Edwards came to my shop one day and said, "Gloria, 'God' told me to tell you to read Psalm 68:4" ["Sing to God, sing praises to His name; Extol Him who rides on the clouds, By His name **YAH**, And rejoice before Him," NKJV]. I was so shocked to see the Name "**YAH**" there was in my King James Bible! God had a name. Just like me and you. I wondered why we were not told his name in church.

Reading the Bible

Somehow, we Christians become blind to the word of 'God' (Father Yah'uah *Elohim*). It is like we don't see words that are right in front of us because we are told, "Read this verse in the Bible." We don't read the Bible like it is a real book. We skip pages and miss lots of words; we don't even realize what we're doing it. It feels like we have been condition not to see the whole truth. We never question what the words really mean because we accept whatever our pastors tell us about the words and the stories in the Bible. There will be a church full of people, but most of them don't bring Bibles; the ones who do have Bibles only open them up. When they are in church but don't always read them at home because they are expecting the pastor to read the passages in church for them. Or we may say, "I cannot read all of those names." in between all of those names there are messages, hidden treasures waiting to be revealed to you, places and people who are playing a very vital part in the Bible. My Bible is the Nelson Study Bible, New King James Version (NKJV). That was the beginning of a true relationship with **"Father Yah'uah"** *Elohim*. We never stop growing in the word every day a new true is revealed to us. First I looked His name up in the dictionary. It said that **"YAH"** was the short form of the defined name of the 'Jewish' 'God' named '*Jehovah.*' Are Yahweh I continue to search the Scriptures in various Bibles and I finally found our

Fathers Yah'uah real name I thought to myself, "I have been grafted into that same 'God' as the Hebrew

Israelites (Father Yah'uah *Elohim*);" I would be one with Him as "*Yah'shua*" is one with Him, I and all of us who believe in the word of 'God' (" **Father Yah'uah**" *Elohim*). We are serving the same *Elohim* as the Hebrews did. " Father **Yah'uah**" *Elohim* is the 'Jewish' people's 'God,' and we have been grafted into their 'Vine,' which is Israel. We serve the same one true Father Yah'uah; I don't know why we were not told these things in church. That was the beginning of my searching for my "Father **Yah'uah**" *Elohim* and my relationship with Him through His only-begotten Son, "*Yah'shua*" the Messiah. I was searching, but I kept coming to a dead ends the pastors kept telling me "That's the 'Jewish' 'God.' Was not our God, and we have nothing to do with them. I thought to myself, that's a lie I was thinking should I tell him he's lying are just search the Scriptures I knew before when I brought truth

People would get mad at me.

'Papa' Curt

Mrs. Tunnage took me to a meeting of the Protestant Women of the Chapel (P.W.O.C.). There I met Gianna Childers who told me about someone who could answer all of my questions about the Hebraic roots of the faith. She gave me the phone number of Dr. Curt Wagner, the husband of Gretchen Wagner, her second cousin (once removed). She addressed him as 'Papa' Curt, and said that they lived in Minnesota. I have 'adopted' them as my spiritual 'parents' since they have been given to me by "**Father Yah'uah**" *Elohim* through "*Yah'shua*" the Messiah. 'Papa' Curt began to teach me everything I could dream of asking him about "**Father Yah'uah**" and "*Yah'shua*" and the Hebrew and Greek scriptures. We would often be on the phone for hours late at night talking about "**Father Yah'uah**" and His Holy Scriptures. If he could not answer a question he would look it up. Many times it would be daybreak before we got off the phone. My mind was always racing with the next question, waiting to hear the next answer. I felt like my whole life had just opened up; I was learning and not being hit or yelled at, and he was not saying, "You won't understand." He took his time to make sure I understood. I was constantly bombarding him with questions and he was always ready to give me answers and let me come up with still more questions. Sometimes I felt like a little girl; I would fall asleep on the telephone. 'Papa' Curt never fussed with me about falling asleep; he would just pick up the next night where we had stopped talking before I fell asleep. If I wanted to know something about any subject he would take the time to answer the question. Although he was not with me physically I felt like he was taking me by the hand, showing me all the wonders of "**Father Yah'uah**." Now that I think about it, it felt like I wasn't a grown lady. I felt like a child when a parent reads a book to him or her; for the first time I was learning. And nobody was calling me stupid because I had so many questions they thought was dumb I asked every question that came to my imagination. Whenever 'Papa' Curt talked with me it seemed like the whole world expanded for me. In he considered none of my questions dumb ones after a while I began to give 'Papa' the answers that I had studied; sometimes I was wrong. I wanted to be right, and like a good father he would talk it out with me and help me find the right answers. He never forced his opinion on me. Yes, he did correct me at times, but he was always willing to help me draw the correct conclusions. I appreciated that part about studying with 'Papa' Curt. Even more than that I loved how he helped me to come to know and fall in love with his 'Heavenly Father,' "**Yah'uah**" our *Elohim*. He helped me to learn how to recognize the still 'voice' of His 'Holy Spirit.' He also helped me to fall in love all over again with His only-begotten Son, "*Yah'shua*" the Messiah. That's what I love most about 'Papa' Curt and his wife, my 'adopted' spiritual father and mother. When we were not studying the Hebrew Scriptures we were talking about outreach to Israel, helping bring 'Jewish people' back to the homeland because I have learned better. They are Hebrew Israelites back to the Land, as well as other missions of helping people all over the globe.

When I met 'Papa' Curt I did not have a place of my own to live in; I was sleeping any place that I could find. Geneva Pitt allowed me to live in her home. When she got ready to leave Georgia it was like separating from one of my children. Geneva is like a daughter to me; when all of the other Christians would not let me live in their homes, Geneva took me in. If she had not, I would have been on the street again. 'Papa' Curt and his wife, Gretchen, were led to donate money to the '**YAH** Gives A Second Chance Ministry' to buy two acres of land and later to buy a triple-wide trailer. That trailer would be used both as a 'parsonage' as well as a place to house people who were struggling to come off drugs and/or were homeless. It still needs a lot of work done to it, but many good people have helped to do so much work on it already. I've only had two men who were not believers who 'ripped me off.' So far it has served its purpose. I work every single day, including Sunday, without pay. I sometimes get up late at night to go get some teenage or baby whose parents were fighting. If the trailer is unavailable I arrange for free hotel housing for strangers or even Christian couples who may be going through divorce. Sometimes it was a soldier who didn't want to go to the barracks because he and/or his spouse were having problems. Men and women, teenagers and children and toddlers, soldiers—white and black—have all stayed here with me.

I'm going to give you a description of what 'Papa' Curt looks like. He is a retired physics professor, but he looks like a mountain man, not a retired scientist. He is nothing like I thought a scientist would look like. I thought that scientists were very distinguished looking people, yet he and his wife love to climb mountains and go for long walks. 'Papa' Curt and his wife both play the violin in the Southwest Minnesota Orchestra. They always act like they have just met each other and fallen in love for the first time. She is very protective of her husband; so is he of his wife. He's always smiling, always happy. He loves life; he finds good in everything and in all people. He loves all people, even the 'worst' people; he'll find something good in them and then he will begin building on that little spark of goodness in them. He makes me laugh when I talk because he does not always understand the meaning of the words I use. I have to explain to him what they mean, even though I'm not using slang. He uses a lot of proper words. He is so willing to understand when I talk to him. 'Papa' Curt has a rough looking beard, so he looks like a mountain man. If you would see him on the street you would not think that he is a scientist. He looks like he is an older 'Jewish' man when he dresses up. He stands about 5'8". When I am disgruntled with someone he finds a way to help me see that they're hurting people too. He finds compassion for them and teaches me to do the same. My 'dad' is the most loving father that **"Father Yah'uah"** could have blessed me with. Everyone calls him 'Papa' Curt; he is everything that a father is supposed to be.

My 'Mother' Gretchen, or 'Mama Curt'

I'm going to give you a description of his wife, my 'mother' Gretchen whom "**Father Yah'uah**" has blessed me with. She is about 5' 11" and I call her 'Mama Curt.' She does not wear any makeup or any kind of jewelry, as she is beautiful on the outside, and extremely beautiful on the inside. She's like a bundle of loving and reasoning and sorting and gathering, explaining, showing, expecting, patiently acknowledging, hoping, and helping you be all that "**Father Yah'uah**" and "*Yah'shua*" want you to be. She feels my joy and she understands my pain. She encourages me in everything I do if it is right before "**Father Yah'uah**." When I do wrong, just as any good mother, she does not hesitate to correct me. She even remembers my birthdays, although we do not celebrate them. She makes sure that I know that I am loved by her, even when I didn't show her the same love I showed to 'Papa' Curt. But she has been so patient with me, and now I love her more than 'Papa' Curt! She has been so patient, even when I had so much anger and hurt. She always acted loving towards me, no matter what. She showed true love, not just the word love; she is love in actions and deeds too. She is the most beautiful person inside and outside; she truly is the essence of "*Yah'shua*" the Messiah because of her love.

Scriptural Mothers and Fathers

I'm going to quote some Scripture from John 19:25–27. "Now there stood by the 'cross' [stake] of 'Jesus' His mother, and His mother's sister, Mary the wife of Clopas, and Mary Magdalene. When 'Jesus' therefore saw His mother, and the disciple whom He loved standing by, He said to His mother, 'Woman, behold your son!' Then He said to the disciple, 'Behold your mother!' And from that hour that disciple took her to his own home." As Christians we do not want to mother and father those who have never experienced mothering and fathering, and full the emptiness that has been in people's lives. When someone comes along in their lives and takes them by the hand they feel as though 'God' has given them a second chance, to know what it feels like to have a mother or father. I can say **"Father Yah'uah"** has truly blessed my life because I have had that chance. Everywhere you turn in the Bible you will find some part of your life that **"Father Yah'uah"** has made real to you. That is one way of finding **"Father Yah'uah,"** because in those scriptures He is revealing who you really are in Him, by giving you revelation of the workings of His 'Holy Spirit.' He reveals His 'Holy Spirit' to you in order to lead you into all truth in all things concerning Himself and His only-begotten Son, *"Yah'shua"* the Messiah. In this way you can become the new man or woman that **"Father Yah'uah"** intended you to be. So as we lay our heavy burdens at the feet of *"Yah'shua"* our deliverer and Father Yah'uah our healer, healing can take place. I know what you're thinking: "I want to let go, I just don't know how to." I've been there so many times. I didn't just fall—I threw myself down! I've been angry about how I was treated for so long that the anger took root within my soul. Satan built a house inside me so his demons would have a place to dwell and to work out all of their schemes of defeat for my life. They had taken up residence, and it was going to be a fight for my life before they would let go, but *"Yah'shua the Messiah"* had already paid the price. So **"Father Yah'uah"** sent His army of people whom he had selected to help me get free through the shed blood of *"Yah'shua the Messiah."* His army was made up of people of all kinds, from every race, rich and poor, young and old; they have had one goal in mind, to set the captive(s) free. That captive person was main.

Rescue from Satan's Demons

Indeed, this harassing by Satan's demons can take place over a period of time; it is the way he destroys who you were intended to be. We have had to learn to do whatever it takes to survive, and most of what we learned to survive on was killing us. We have the right, the absolute right, to be angry, to be mad about the situation. All it was doing was killing us; it distorts who we really are supposed to be. It is a day-by-day process of choosing not to be angry—and trust me it is not an easy process—and sometimes when you see the same thing repeating itself, it makes it worse. But you have to understand that it is Satan's plan to destroy us; it is our choice to fight for our salvation and maintain the territory that "**Father Yah'uah**" has given us. So many times we are just like Adam and Eve, or Esau; we hand over our birthrights to Satan without even a fight, just for the chance to feel sorry for ourselves or to gain the riches of this world. We think no one loves us and that we are always on the losing team. We do not see the things that Satan's demons are producing in us. These are the things that anger produces: anxiety, nervousness, confusion, and mental problems; suicidal thoughts and violence to others; no ambition, no feelings, and no consciousness of others; fear of yourself and others; and no recognition of yourself or others. You don't feel like you are a real person because you are constantly hating and discrediting people and always thinking how to get back at someone so that you are constantly fighting with others. You are never forgetting, never forgiving, never letting go of the past, but always plotting, always lying, always hiding. You are always denying the existence of 'Jesus Christ' ("*Yah'shua*" the Messiah) by accusing Him of not loving you and of letting everything happen to you, saying that "**Father Yah'uah**" is not a just 'God' (*Elohim*). You are never trusting in the Messiah to lead you to faith in "**Father Yah'uah**" *Elohim* or in anything or anyone. You are never having any real happiness and only short-lived relationships with others because you desire always to be alone, all the time isolated from the world. You are always being the victim, never taking any real responsibility for your actions and never wanting any real truth to come into your life. You are always blaming others for your actions and so you are experiencing no real victory. You are never able to make reasonable choices, constantly commanding and condemning yourself and others in your life. As a result you have constant confusion in thinking about death and self-pity; this is the actual 'death sentence' that Satan has planned out for you. Scripture says in Romans 12:2: "And do not be conformed to this world, but be transformed by the renewing of your mind, that you may prove what is that good and acceptable and perfect will of 'God.'"

Overcoming Evil

Here are some other Scriptures that will give you strength to evict Satan's demons and evil spirits from your being. Deuteronomy 16:20: "You shall follow what is altogether just, that you may live and inherit the land which 'the LORD' ["**Father Yah'uah**"] your 'God' [*Elohim*] is giving you." First Corinthians 13:4: "Love suffers long and is kind; love does not envy; love does not parade itself, is not puffed up." Philippians 4: 8–9: "Finally, brethren, whatever things are true, whatever things are noble, whatever things are just, whatever things are pure, whatever things are lovely, whatever things are of good report, if there is any virtue and if there is anything praise-worthy— meditate on these things. The things which you learned and received and heard and saw in me, these do, and the 'God' (Father Yah'uah) of peace will be with you." Romans 15:33: "Now the 'God' (Farher Yah'uah) of peace be with you all. Amen." And Ephesians 4:25–27: "Therefore, putting away lying, let each one of you speak truth with his neighbor, for we are members of one another. Be angry, and do not sin; do not let the sun go down on your wrath, nor give place to the devil."

My Family, Continued

What 'Papa' and 'Mama Curt' wanted was more than just to make sure that I had a place to live in physically or a ministry to run. They wanted to see me completely healed in my mind and my spirit; they were not compromising. They were not quiet about it either. When I made mistakes or when I fell short of the glory of **"Father Yah'uah"** *Elohim* they knew they had a job on their hands. No matter what behavior I displayed they 'rolled up their sleeves' and got to work with the authority of *"Yah'shua"* and all of his weapons of warfare. And the greatest weapon that they had was His love. They continue as good parents in their love, to keep me on track and going in the direction that **"Father Yah'uah"** wills for my life. That is a description of the love of **"Father Yah'uah"** that was displayed in my 'adopted' parents toward me. When we are born we do not choose our father in mother. If we are adopted we do not choose our father and mother. But I was so blessed because **"Father Yah'uah"** *Elohim* let me choose my 'adopted' parents!

I want to talk about Ms. Inez Powell; she is one of my sisters in *"Yah'shua."* She is always protecting me; she will not let me get too far off the track and then says, "Hey, it is time to come in now." I love her with the love of **"Father Yah'uah"** *Elohim* for all the good things she does for me and the things she brings into my life. She knows I can preach; whenever I ask her to attend one of the functions where I am preaching she is always there to support me. She always expects a code of conduct out of me and she refuses to let me feel sorry for myself. She will even make me preach her a whole sermon over the phone; by the time I'm finished both of us are praising "**Father Yah'uah**." She cares when I'm sick, and she's the first person <u>here with</u>. I needed medicine for me on a regular basis. She goes shopping for food for me. She refuses to let me go with her, because I try to get the cheapest things I can find on the shelf such as no-name brands and marked-down food items and out-of-date food. I will put them in the shopping cart but she'll take them out of the shopping cart. So now she will never let me shop with her. She makes sure that all the food is not out-of-date and things that are nutritional and healthy are there for me every day. She calls me and fusses with me if I don't answer the phone. She is bossy in a 'big-sister' way, but always in a loving way. She will remind me of how I treat people and how I make sure that the homeless I serve have the very best that I could afford, never giving them stuff that I would be ashamed of. Miss Inez reminds me that I deserve the very best; just as I feel about my clients that is how she feels about me.

Miss Patricia Moore is another one of my sisters through the blood of "*Yah'shua*." When Patricia's mother was sick I went to Douglas, Georgia, to help take care of her until she went home to be with "**Father Yah'uah**" *Elohim*. I went without pay and stayed as long as I could, and as often as I could be there for the family, whenever Patricia needed me. She made sure from that day on that she was no longer just a friend but a sister. She treats me as though I'm one of her family. No matter what she does for me, she never throws it up in my face. She never makes me ask for her help. She just helps me and when I try to pay her back she reminds me that when she needed me, I was there for her entire family. That is the only thing she ever throws up in my face. She is like a sister who is real close to me and who will spoil me like I'm her real Baby sister. Patricia is a schoolteacher who teaches kindergarten, so she has a lot of patience with me. One time she said, "Gloria, you are just like my kids at school; I have to have lots of patience with you." Patricia and Ms. Inez refuse to let me believe that I am alone.

I am part of a big family. I have lots of brothers and sisters. Mr. and Mrs. Bunn and their daughter, Miss Sylvia Jones, are very good friends of mine. Sylvia and I are like rival sisters; we are always fighting for the attention of Mr. Bunn. Mrs. Bunn is like 'Big Mom.' She keeps the family together, and I'm part of that family. When we are together I follow Mrs. Bunn all over the house, asking her all kinds of questions and touching all the antiques in her home. Sylvia makes sure I always have vitamins because my nails were turning black as a result, of having vitamin deficiency. Sylvia purchases my vitamins and sends them to Georgia from Virginia. She does other good things for me and for other people. Sylvia has a big heart; she is always reaching out towards people. Although I fuss with her at times I know she loves me and will do anything to help make my life better, and not only my life but the life of anyone who comes into her presence. I started out with a suitcase full of horror, but now look at what **"Father Yah'uah"** *Elohim* and *"Yah'shua"* the Messiah have done in my life! I am now a part of a loving and caring Christian family, with a father, mother, sisters, and brothers. There are a lot of them who are willing to put on the whole armor of **"Father Yah'uah"** *Elohim* to be the voice, the hands and legs in the heart of Father Yah'uah to bring change into my life. I am so grateful.

My son feels like I was never a good mother. He is right. I was not. So I decided I was not going to let him manipulate me into feeling bad about the only decisions I knew how to make for his life and mine at that time. I usually get so upset I cry for days or shut down, especially when he says, "You have never done anything for me." You never love me I did, and I still do love my children. However I am refusing now to let anyone, including my own children, take me away from the love of **"Father Yah'uah"** and His only-begotten Son, *"Yah'shua"* the Messiah. **"Father Yah'uah"** has a way of bringing families back together if we allow him to, and I believe one day that **"Father Yah'uah"** will heal my son and he will be able to forgive me. I hope that one day my son will be able to love beyond all of his hurt. That's my hope that Lesroy will find it in his heart to forgive me for what I did when I did not know nor understand how to be a real mother.

Children in 'Christ'

There are a lot of young people in my life. Some are very hardheaded and some are children who need to be loved. **"Father Yah'uah"** has blessed me to have Ms. Shiela Rice. Shiela is younger than my daughter Monique, about six years younger. Her personality is very giving and very loving. She experienced a lot of disappointments and hurt in her life but she turned it around and she keeps a positive attitude about things going on in her life. She is actually a joy to have as a daughter. **"Father Yah'uah"** made her such a loving person, always ready to lend anybody a helping hand. Shiela comes over and anything I need she tries to make sure I have, just as my daughter Monique does. But most important of all is the time she spends with me. Anyone who cannot love Shiela will miss out on a lot of love.

Her husband, Mr. Roger Rice, is the son that my son refuses to be; Mr. Rice treats me like I'm his mom. Sometimes when I go to his computer shop I touch everything because I love computers. He never says a word. I look at the software, pick up pieces to computers, and just touch all the 'stuff.' When I come to see Mr. Rice he lets me watch him work on computers. He donates computers. To my clients who cannot afford computers Mr. Rice gives me tower, monitor, keyboard, mouse, and speakers. The looks on the faces of the children, the tears I have seen coming down a mother's cheeks, her eyes red from joy that someone cared about her and her children! You should see the screaming and jumping over a used computer. But Mr. Rice makes sure when he gives me a computer. It is in very good condition and has all the latest software on it. Then the child does not even think that it is a used computer. Mr. Rice never gets the chance to meet the families he's helping or has blessed with the computers, people of every color and nationality, men and women coming out of jail trying to start a business, children just going to college—Mr. Rice gives them their start in life. It is only the love of "**Father Yah'uah**" through "*Yah'shua*" that allows him to be this generous and still maintains his business. He never says 'no' to me. He's been doing this with me now for about eight years, maybe longer. I tell him about the family's history and why they cannot afford a computer—most of the time they are single mothers who just need someone to help them. The excitement and joy on their faces he never sees. Maybe it is what Mr. Rice sees on my face; in a quiet way he says that his pay comes from *Elohim*. He gets not a thank-you and no rewards, just the joy of knowing he has helped another family obtain a computer. His doing of good things for others is enough of a reward for him. As a result I can truly say that Roger and Shiela Rice, Geneva Pitts, Evelyn Byrd, and a whole host of others are also my 'children' through the shed blood of the Messiah *Yah'shua*.

My Computers

There are eight computers in my house. This is where the children that people think cannot learn to use computers come. Some of them are mentally challenged, but **"Father Yah'uah"** allows me to teach them too, and Mr. Rice makes sure that the computers are always working. He never complains, "I just fixed that computer." He knows that I let the adults and children use the computers. He knows that spending a lot of time working with the disabled will mean you are going to have some issues with your computers. A lot of the issues come from me, too; I'm always going places on the Internet I should not go and downloading things I should not. Mr. Rice keeps these computers working. Some of them, well almost all of them, Mr. Rice had given to me originally. Had it not been for him I would not have been able to complete this book, because of the special software that I needed for the computer. He has to program the computer for me and then I have to learn to use the new software. I will call him and say, "Mr. Rice, I did not touch anything." He knows in his heart I was touching everything, but he never scolds me or gets mad at me and he never calls me stupid. He says, "I know you are learning to use the software." Those words give me so much more comfort and support to venture into the unknown. He pushes every bit of my curiosity to learn more about the computer and the things I desire to do or complete. I could not complete this book without his giving me a brand new computer with much fast memory on it. My 'son' Mr. Rice did this for me. He knew how important it was for me to complete this book so he built me a computer, and Mr. Rice and Sheila make it a lifestyle of helping people. I love them both as my real 'children.' I have almost 20 pages of other 'children' that **"Father Yah'uah"** has blessed me with, and all of them have unique personalities that make them special. They come to check on me and to make sure I am okay, and I love each one of them and their personalities in a different way. They are all very special people to me.

Others that I consider sisters are Mattie Brown and Shineka Patterson. We call Mattie 'Mutt.' Mattie really is such a good friend. I like talking to 'Mutt;' she has me laughing the whole time when we are talking and she always lets me have my moments. Together they run a daycare, and 'Mutt' lets me help. I had the children so spoiled that she did not want anyone to help her but me.

I wanted to give you a chance to see the many kinds of people in my life. I have been so blessed to have them all in my life. There are even more people, but I cannot tell all the different things they do in this one book.

My Doctor

Dr. Seth Borquaye is one of the very special people in my life. He is a doctor who operated on me to remove the ugly scar tissue and the deformity that was between my legs caused by the abuse that went on in Mama's house. I was hung up in the ceiling of the basement and hooks were attached to my private parts. The weight of my body from the hooks being attacked to my vagina caused it to be disfigured so it had ugly scar tissue hanging from it. When I first went to him and asked him if he would operate on me he said to me, "If it's not hurting you it's not necessary." It wasn't hurting me, but it was a constant reminder of what had happened to me and those scars were ugly. I do not know if it was the pain and the anguish or the shame that he saw on my face and the hurt that he heard in my voice. It would be two years later that he would walk into my shop and ask me, "Do you still want that operation?" I said "yes" so he operated and fixed me.

I'm going to give you a description of Dr. Seth Borquaye. He is a tall man, kind of slender; he is from Africa. He has a beautiful accent, and from seeing the pictures on his desk of his wife and children I know that he is married. How he looks at those pictures with pride to have them as his family shows you that he is happily married and thankful to be a father. He is one of the friendliest Christians you would ever want to meet. He is the type of doctor that listens to you and discusses the problems with you. He never sends you away feeling like he thinks "he know everything about you, because I've seen this problem so many times." He listens carefully to what you have to say and then he checks you out and tells you his findings. That is rare in doctors today. Because I am not able to tell the doctors how much pain I am in, they think I'm making things up. When I'm asked, "Where are you hurting?" I can't tell them. So I've been accused of being on drugs until they run tests and find out they're wrong and there's something really wrong with me. Once when I had gastric bypass surgery I was put into a mental hospital until they realized all my vitals were shutting down. They had to put an intravenous tube in my neck for feeding me because all of my veins in my arms had collapsed. My arm had been broken in two places in a car accident in New York City. While in the hospital the doctors called the police officer into the room with me. He said he believed I was on some type of drugs, because I was oblivious to the fact that my arm was broken in two places. I was not oblivious; I just couldn't feel any pain. I was not in shock; I just didn't feel the pain. My mind shut down, and I was seeing things through the eyes of a child. Again the doctor said to me that he had seen only one other person like me. Most of the time, because I cannot explain what was wrong to the doctors or nurses, they think there is nothing wrong with me most of the time I am still eating and drinking, smiling and talking. I have gone to the hospital and they said that nothing was wrong, so they decided to send me back home. And then I think that I needed some air so I decided to go outside, at which time I just passed out in the street and had to be hospitalized. Then the doctors found out themselves that something was extremely wrong with me. Before that they were rude to me because I could not explain to them what was really wrong.

Right now there is something wrong with my digestive system. You can smell my bowels in my breath because of the gastric bypass surgery; it is hard for people to be around me. The doctors have told me it is a gum disease, but the dentists say it is not. The only way that I'm able to function at all is because of my taking prenatal vitamins that Sylvia sends me; it helps my nails turn from black to their natural color. Without the vitamins I become so sick sometimes I cannot stand up; I have to take the pills at least four times a day. My blood pressure gets out of whack, because I cannot go to the bathroom without taking all kinds of laxatives. I can go for up to a month without going to the bathroom. When I try to tell the doctors this they don't believe me, so my body gets used to the different laxatives I have to take—whatever I can get my hands on. Those are the worst times for me; I am always afraid that something will be wrong with me and the hospital will let me die because I can't show the proper emotions for pain. I thank "**Father Yah'uah**" *Elohim* for Dr. Borquaye because he took the time to listen to me and get to know me as a patient and an individual person. Dr. Borquaye acts just like a regular person; his status as a doctor has not gone to his head and the love he shows with each patient is so extremely beautiful. He also runs an orphanage in Africa. He helps in the general community and surrounding areas of Hinesville, Georgia he helps a lot of the different organizations by physically being present and supporting them in so many different ways. That's what he did with me. He was physically my doctor; he was spiritually helpful to me to change people's lives that came into 'The Heart of Christ, Inc.' and he gave donations of clothing and other types of support to keep the ministry running smoothly. He is my friend through "*Yah'shua*;" that's what one of my brothers did to help me in our community he allowed me to represent him through The Heart of Christ to help people that were in need.

My Attorney

Attorney Robert Pirkle is one of the most respected persons in our community. Mr. Pirkle doesn't act like he is an important person in the community. When he walks around town when he sees you, no matter who he is with, he will speak to you. When people say "hello" he will want to know how you are doing; he always leaves you feeling like you are the important one. He acts like I'm on a mission from *Elohim* all the time. I think he is thinking, "I'm going to bring change in someone's life today." He is not an attorney just for the money; he really does all he can do for people. He really believes he's just a regular person like you or me. What I mean by that is Mr. Pirkle will get on any level to understand what he's doing for you and how best to represent you. I remember when I was trying to get my tax-exempt status and my 501(c)(3) [which is provides for charitable organizations to receive tax-deductible contributions] for 'The Heart of Christ, Inc.' I went to about eight lawyers that day and I had to walk everywhere I went because at that time I did not know how to drive. Mr. Pirkle was the ninth lawyer. He listened to me about the vision that I have for 'The Heart of Christ, Inc.' There was one problem—I did not have the money to pay him. He said to me, "You come up with $800 and I will do the rest." I came up with $600 and he did the rest. He said, "You do not owe me a thing." At that time, everything he did for 'The Heart of Christ, Inc.' was without charge. He's only charged me one time for representing me in court when I got a DUI. He knew I was going through a terrible time with my Christian walk with *Elohim* and the people of the church, but that was no excuse for me to get behind the steering wheel of a car drinking. All the other times he did not charge me, not even for any personal work; just those three times and the time he did the paperwork for our land purchase. And he has done a lot of work for me. A lot of my clients could not pay him all at once. He would charge a very low fee and sometimes no fee at all. He shows the love of *Yah'shua* the Messiah in everything he does; he has helped so many people in our community. He doesn't boast about it, he doesn't tell it; he just does it because he is an attorney for *Elohim* first. I believe he helps my clients because I have asked him to, but I also believe that even if I didn't ask him and someone came to him on their own, just like I did, he would help them to. I believe this is so because of the love he shows for the people of our *Elohim* for the people in our community. He is a very blessed man. The things I like about him the most is that he's not afraid of 'getting his hands dirty' to work hard in our community, and that he thinks of himself as just a 'regular Joe.' He can meet any challenge head-on.

Clay and Tracy Sikes

I met Mr. and Mrs. Clay and Tracy Sikes at church. Everybody thought I was so difficult but Clay did not. He knew some emotional things were going on in my life although I did not say so. When they wanted to kick me out of church he spoke up on my behalf that had never happened before in my life. Tracy and Clay invited me to their house. He taught me a lot about peoples' character and he guided me in a lot of projects that were going on at 'The Heart of Christ, Inc.'; he helped me make good decisions. He didn't impress his ideas on me; he helped me make the best decision I could with the people I was serving. He worked side-by-side with me on so many projects and when he could not he would advise me. I don't see a lot of Clay now but he will make time for me when I need to talk to him. Clay has helped feed the homeless in our county and the surrounding counties. He has prayed with so many people and ministered to many. He has helped men and women get jobs, even hiring them, and seeing that any disadvantaged children helping to education our children in our community. I am not just talking about his wife, I'm talking about his whole family, mother, father, brothers, sisters, cousins, uncles, aunts, nephews and nieces. Even his children are all dedicated to making a big impact on the disadvantaged. No matter where Clay goes he touches someone's life, rich and poor alike. He is no respecter of persons—everybody deserves a chance. He touched my life and so many others' lives. I had the pleasure of meeting a lot of Clay's family members, but the one that stands out the most to me is Gill Sikes. Just like Clay, Gill has done so much for people. Gill really loves people. Even though you can see a lot of hurting in him, he's always ready to do something good for someone. Gill has helped me so much with people of every race and denomination. Gill has a way of touching the heart of everybody that he comes in contact with. Sometimes when Gill is talking to me it seems like he's acknowledging me as his parent, like a son talking to his mother. I feel that way when Gill is talking to me; it is the soft tone that a son uses when he is talking to his mother. He is like a son showing his mother new ideas without offending her, or showing her a new way to look at a situation. That really touches my heart. One of the men who worked on this trailer was ripping me off big time and Gill did not hesitate to let me know this man was doing it. He still was so gentle when he talked to me, advising me how to handle the situation, even though he had so much going on with his business. When his mother-in-law passed away he and his wife still found time to help other people. I love Gill and his wife Nikki. Their whole family is truly dedicated in changing the lives of others.

Dr. Deborah Rodriguez, a close friend of Nikki's family, asked me if I would pray with Nikki's mother, Mrs. Wanda Wells. I said yes, and off we went to another county. When I got there, what I saw will be with me for the rest of my life. Family and friends and loved ones, people who cared about her, were there. It did not seem like I did not belong there. It was as if they were all waiting for me to come home, like I was a part of that big family. Deborah Tunnage and I were the only black people in the room but we were treated with so much love, so much tenderness, as though it was our family member who was leaving. When she saw me, she looked at me with those big beautiful hazel-green eyes. A smile came on her face and she said, "Here is my black angel. I've been waiting for you to come." She said that 'God' (*Elohim*) showed me to her in a vision. She wasn't sorry about knowing she was going home to be with *Elohim*. She only wanted to celebrate her life with family and friends who had been a blessing to her. We sang songs and praised Elohim, and she pronounced blessings over me that day. I had come to pray for her, but she prayed for me first, then she said that 'God' had told her to do this. Mrs. Wanda has marked my soul. I will always have a place in my heart for her children and husband. She said that I would never be without people to love me. I wonder sometimes, "How did she know I felt like no one loved me most of the time?" I felt people just used me for what they needed from me, but with those big, beautiful hazel-green eyes, with her love, her spirit surrounded my very soul with the love of Father Yah'uah she will be with me for the rest of my life. I made two more visits before she went home to be with "**Father Yah'uah.**" On my last visit she gave me a check to help take care of people, and when she passed away one of her close friends gave me another check. Even on her deathbed she continued to take care of people she allowed me to be an ambassador for her to this day her children, especially Nikki, call me, always wanting to know what they can do to change someone's life. I am the most unlikely person to have so many loving and good people in my life. Who does not see race or my education, not even my background they are able to love me. I had to take my eyes off of those who could not love me and see *"Yah'shua"* in those who could love me. I had to see how many loved me because of the heart of *"Yah'shua the Messiah."* There was no race or denomination, no rich, no poor, just people changing my life and changing the lives of others. *"Yah'shua* touches people through the hearts of people like these; I am just their representative. Like an ambassador, I have represented the city of Hinesville. It was not just me alone. It was so many different faces, so many different races, and so many different nationalities. It wasn't church or denomination; it was Father Yah'uah humble love through his people.

The Newspaper Editor

One of the most just men I have ever met is the editor of the Coastal Courier, our local newspaper in Hinesville. Mr. Pat was so fair in publishing stories about me and 'The Heart of Christ, Inc.' He knew that there are always two sides of a story. He let people know what was going on in our community and in all of the organizations that dealt with people. He would put my articles in the paper just as I wrote them. He is such a true blessing to our community, and I have so much respect for him. It's amazing how **"Father Yah'uah"** puts all the right people in all the right places to carry out his plan we think it is us but is not it is Father Yah'uah assess people through us we do not have to go around saying, "I do this in the name of 'Jesus' (*"Yah'shua"*)." I think you have to live your life according to the words of *"Father Yah'uah.* When you care for any of the disadvantaged of the world and speak out for the oppressed **"Father Yah'uah"** will bless you in ways that you cannot always understand. Because I was willing to be an ambassador, for all of the people of Hinesville who-wanted to be a blessing to others So now I am being a blessed also.

The Dating World

I decided to have gastric bypass surgery. As a result I went from 287 pounds to 130 pounds and from a size 26 to a size 7 dress. So no matter where I went heads turned. About eight months earlier I had been engaged to a chaplain, but I've never told anybody completely what happened to me, not even him. A Christian counselor who had worked with me for some years helped me with the ministry that I ran, and we did ministry with people together. I didn't find out until later that he played a big part in why the chaplain made his decision not to marry me. I really can't blame it on him because it was the chaplain's decision. When the chaplain had asked him if I would make a good wife his response was, "No, she would not" instead of telling him he needed to discuss his issues with me. So he played a big part in helping to dissolve the relationship I had with this chaplain. Besides he was in a relationship with another woman in the same church and I knew nothing about it. He used what the counselor had told him to make his excuse to marry another lady.

So I separated myself from Christians and other friends, another trap in another scheme that Satan uses to take me out of the will of *Elohim*. In all the studying and all the reading I had done I had not learned how to stand when Satan brings attacks, one after another. I went back to my 'vomit'- what I knew best: the night club and losing myself on the dance floor [See Pr. 26:11: "As a dog returns to his own vomit, so a fool repeats his folly."]. I walked away from the only people and the only *Elohim* who were protecting me; I traded that protection for two DUIs. I had come into agreement with the devil that I was nothing, that I would never be anything, and I would never have anything. I began to go to nightclubs and dance most of the time. When I left the nightclub I would have all kinds of telephone numbers. The funny thing is that I never called any of them. Dancing was my way of escaping from reality, and drinking was an easy way of helping me to be able to talk to the people that I was out with. Drinking made it easy for me to be around people and do my 'ungodly' things. I did not go by myself; a group of ladies and I went to the nightclub and men would buy me all kinds of drinks. The ladies that I went with were happy because that meant they would have drinks. Often when ladies go out together the one who gets the most drinks usually doesn't drink them all. The friends at the table get to drink the drinks and I get the guys to buy them. Then I say "I want to dance," and the guy says, "Let's go dance." So the drinks stay on the table and the friends at the table get to drink my drinks. We knew before we went out that that was the plan. I knew how to play this game too well. Everybody gets what they want to drink free, including me. Now that I look at it in hindsight, the guys were really paying to dance with me by providing me with drinks. I stayed on the dance floor until the club closed, only coming off briefly when I needed another drink, or I got hot and needed some air, or I had to go to the restroom, or one of my girlfriends gave me the signal that she needed a drink. I was just turning fifty-five years old, but no one knew my age by looking at me. Once I put on my 'war paint' (makeup) and my 'weebie-weebie' (hair weave), tight-fitting clothes, and high heels, I was thinking my pear shape looked like a million. Nobody could tell me anything. I knew I was not beautiful, and certainly not even pretty, but the way I was built was what attracted men to me. I knew that, so I used it to my advantage. And I was a very good dancer. Sometimes when my friends would see me dancing they would be shocked and in total disbelief. Everything that MTV girls could do I knew how to do them too. I watched people dance on TV about ten minutes, and then I was off doing the very same thing, every raunchy move, not missing a beat. No matter who else was dancing, all eyes would be on me. There had been times when my girlfriends would be angry with me because some guy they wanted to talk to wanted to talk to me and I would not give them the time of day. So my girlfriends thought I was stuck up or a tease. I probably was both, but it was my world and I controlled everything in it, or so I thought. Actually no matter where I was, **"Father Yah'uah"** my *Elohim* was there too, even if I made my bed in hell (Psalm 139:7–8). No matter where I was, He was there too, waiting for me to come back to my senses and into His presence.

Suddenly I was brought back into the real world. One night when we were out 'clubbing' a young lady had cut her wrists because her husband was killed in Iraq. Everyone was screaming and running around like crazy people. When I saw the blood I tore a piece of my slip off and wrapped it around her wrists and began praying to *Father Yah'uah in the name of Yahshua the Messiah* to save her. I went to the hospital with her, and then kept her children until she came home. She became a Christian and I came off the streets. I knew that no matter how far I tried to run from **"Father Yah'uah"** my *Elohim*, I could not. He had let me go back into the world, but the moment tragedy came I returned back to **"Father Yah'uah"** without even thinking about it. He had made Himself a strong part of who I was really supposed to be. I could not separate myself from **"Father Yah'uah,"** even though I thought I wanted to. When hard things come, without thinking you can sense **"Father Yah'uah"** your *Elohim* with you. He never leaves you; He never forsakes you (Hebrews 13: 5). It is always us who go looking for other gods in their pleasures that have nothing to do with the Kingdom of Father Yah'uah and the King of Kings. After that I started praying again and I stopped going to nightclubs.

The Last Man I Married

One day a friend of mine said, "Hey, you need to have somebody permanent in your life." I thought, "She's right, I do need someone permanent in my life" because I wasn't getting any younger. I still did not know how to be in love. I knew how to be a servant to a man, but only in the sense of doing whatever made him happy; it had nothing to do with being in love with him. So once again I put my plans together without including "**Father Yah'uah**." I had my girlfriend create a web page for me on one of the dating sites, and that is where I met my husband about two months after going on that website. I started too talked to all kinds of men. I knew that I wanted an older gentleman between 60 and 69 years old, very caring and very loving, who would put "**Father Yah'uah**" and "*Yah'shua*" first and would be committed to his church and his wife. I wanted him to be a carpenter who loved to sing and who would work out problems with his wife. I also wanted him to be patient and understanding of every situation and to help me run the ministry. I wanted him to help me to be 'godly' and to make 'godly' decisions, and I wanted him to be in the relationship for the long haul. I never mentioned anything about me wanting to be in love with him because I knew I was incapable of showing or giving him that kind of love, but I knew I would be faithful and respectful to him. I wanted him to be about 6'1" tall, light skin, and gray or brown eyes, and that is almost exactly what I got. Satan always feeds your lust of the flesh. I did not labor in prayer; I just said to my-self and to my girlfriend, "This is what I want". Never once did I include my

Messiah "*Yah'shua*" or the Holy Spirit in what I wanted, so my girlfriend and I set out to find my husband on the Internet.

We are going to call him Mr. 'Bob,' me and my girlfriend went on the computer for about a month, and then we started talking on the phone to different men that we thought would be a good candidate for me if I was at work. She would interview the man like she was me. I finally found one that we thought was good enough for me. He asked me if he could come down to visit me; at that time we had only been talking on the phone for about two months. But now I was afraid of meeting him in person because I knew he would be more interested in how I was built rather than in me as a person. I discussed it with my girlfriend and we decided to let him come for a visit.

My outfit was absolutely beautiful and my shoes were simply gorgeous. Everything I had on was beautiful and very appropriate. He was coming and I was ready with my girlfriend on standby to call me every thirty minutes to make sure he was on his best behavior. And he was—at first. I loved to hear his stories about history and places and things in nature, about science and different countries, but most of all about the Bible. And I love music. He sang with a group of older gentlemen—it was more like a barbershop quartet—and a lot of classical music. He said he was an engineer at an Army base, and did contract work for the military. He was also a deacon in a church that he attended regularly. He had all the qualifications I was looking for.

We dated for another two months. He visited me most of the time; I never met any of his friends or family. He would come down and stay in a hotel or in another room at Geneva's home, but we did not have sex. He told me a lot about himself, and I told him what I wanted him to know about me. I did tell him that I saw a psychologist every now and then because of some emotional problems. He said he was so proud of me because I was dealing with my issues. He wanted me to talk about some of them with him so he could see where he needed to be a help to me. I was not in love, but I was in a daze. I was truly captivated by him, but I was relentless in not telling him my secrets. I only told him basic things that he needed to know. I told him that my mother used her children as prostitutes. That was really too much information for him, but I never went into any details.

I said it was his choice if he wanted to continue to see me. He said, "Yes I do! All of that was in your past, and you were a baby and a young child when that went on. Who you are today is a wonderful beautiful person." There that word was again (beautiful). He was very educated, and he knew all the right things to say to me the things I longed to hear. He knew so much about so many different things in life that he could hold a great conversation on any topic with anyone. When he was talking to me about any subject his voice captivated my mind. He reminded me of some type of college professor and he dressed very distinguished. Whenever he talked everyone in the room listened because he knew so much about whatever conversation he was having with you.

Sometimes when we were around people I kept quiet, because I was ashamed of his having someone that was not his equal. When he asked me why I withdrew from him and people like I did, I would respond to him in this manner: "What you need to do is get someone in your life that is intelligent like you." He responded like this to me: "Gloria, you are one of the most intelligent young ladies I have ever met; you are compassionate about what you do; you are- loving towards others. You help bring purpose to my life, and I need you in my life." Wow! He knocked me completely off my feet. I was tiptoeing in my high heels! Never had I ever heard such words concerning me. For the first time a man saw the real me, not the shape of my body. He was constantly telling me how beautiful I was, and he wanted me to stop looking at the floor when I talked with him or other people. He said, "You have nothing to keep your head hung down for."

I could not see him for what he really was because his words were so captivating like Eve his words sound real good to me. I began to relax and allow him to hold my hand, from handholding to kissing to petting. He wanted to be with me sexually, but I said, "No, if you want me you would have to marry me." I still was not in love with him. A couple of days later I began to see different images of him, especially when he tried hugging me or kissing me. It was as though I was seeing different ladies' faces on his face, or feeling the presence of other women once when this happen I went into seizures it was so many images flooding my mind and so many different sense of perfumes. I went to my girlfriend at her workplace and I said, "I need to talk to you." [This was a totally different woman from the one who helped me create the web page; this was a 'born-again' Christian woman]. I told her what I was feeling and seeing. She explained to me, "You are just afraid of being romantically involved with him." She said, "I'm pretty sure he had other women in his life before meeting you; talk to him about what you're feeling." So I did. I said, "'Bob,' every time you hug and kiss me I see different women I told him I could even smell there perfume. Especially when you pull me close to you I can feel their presence." He asked me, "Is that why you pull away from me all the time?" I wanted to be truthful, so I said "yes." Then he told me: "The enemy (meaning Satan) does not want to see you happy, so he is conjuring up all of these accusations in your mind against me. Haven't I been good to you? I want you to trust me. I have had other girlfriends, but you are the one I want to marry." I said to him: "I'm sorry I told you I had a lot of emotional things going on in my life; can you forgive me?" At first he seemed to be very upset with my even bringing such foolishness to him. But I begged and pleaded with him to forgive me for my stupid and outrageous behavior. He said he wanted to go home so he could clear his head and think about what he wanted to do, because he knew I really wanted to marry him without us getting any older. But if I could not trust him, then he said he needed to think about us being together.

I didn't hear from him for about a week, we usually talk on the phone every day. I was so miserable. I was hurting inside. That was a new feeling for me and I missed him. When he called, he started off by saying: "Well honey, you know how I feel about you, but I know that if you can't trust me then we do not need to see each other anymore. I know I love you but this is best for both of us." I started crying and said "okay." We hung up the phone. About five minutes later he called me back. He wanted to know if I was really crying. He wanted me to explain to him why I was crying. I told him my feelings were hurting me. He asked me if I wanted him to come to Georgia. I told him I didn't know what I wanted. He asked the question again, and I said "yes." So he drove down to see me that evening. Instead of his sleeping in a separate room from me that night we slept in the same bed; he slept on top of the covers and I slept underneath the covers.

It normally takes about three hours to drive from where he lived to where Geneva's house is. But he was there in an hour. It didn't dawn on me until a couple of days later, but I had sensed that he was already on his way. He had just wanted it to be my idea, for me to stay calm. Sometimes we want something or someone so bad that we become blind to all the warning signs. The more time we spent together, the more I felt like something was going on, but I was afraid to confront him again. He already knew about the operation that Dr. Borquaye was going to perform on me. So he wanted to be married before the operation, and I said "No." We had already begun kissing, hugging and arousing each other without having sex. I would begin to shut down every time. So I went to my friend at her job again and told her my feelings. She said to me: "When you get out of the hospital, you need to go stay with him a couple of days and meet his family and friends." I had talked to his daughter a few times over the phone and prayed with her; she was very ill and was in and out of the hospital. She was such a pleasant young lady, very respectful and very nice. When I finally met her (not until after we were married) I saw that she was beautiful and very polite, easy to talk to. She was just concerned about our happiness. When I stayed at his house we stayed in separate bedrooms. We spent a lot of time watching television. I don't know the proper word to use so I am going to simply say—we 'made out' most of the time. He spent time fussing at me because I did not want to actually have intercourse. We had agreed to wait before actually having sex, but we did other things. Whenever I said I did not want to go so far, he would always remind me that we were going to be married. So I would submit to some of the things he wanted us to do whenever it would become difficult for me to say no.

I started to have seizures again. He said I was just tired, that I needed something to calm me down. "Maybe you need to talk to your psychologist." I made an appointment with Dr. Richard Anderson, but I don't think I talked to him at all about 'Bob.' I was good at hiding things from Dr. Anderson, although I wanted him to help me. I don't know why I wanted to hide things from one of the best persons; Father Yah'uah had put in my life. Sometimes when I would go to see him I was thinking "Don't give him any ammunition to use against you later." I was afraid to tell him about 'Bob.' It may have been because the other counselor had told everything he knew about me to the chaplain, and I didn't want that to happen again. That had caused me so much distress. I looked at what one person did, with his telling my personal business, and all sorts of things that has made it impossible for me to trust even Dr. Richard Anderson. I lost trust for the one person who had stood by me, who had told me I wasn't crazy, who had told me why I perceive things differently than other people. Not only did Dr. Anderson tell me what was wrong with me, but also he urged me to read books so that I could understand why I didn't feel pain or I saw things in a different way than other people. He helped me understand how I was able to work out other people's problems and how I was able to do things differently that I had no knowledge of, but the spirit of distress had already set in. I did go, but I didn't talk. I was being manipulative, so that when 'Bob' asked me if I had gone to see the psychologist I could say "Yes."

I asked 'Bob' if we could wait a year before we got married. He said, "I do not want to wait a year for the woman I love." He said to me, "I know that you do not love me, but you will grow to love me." I was thinking, "I've had to learn to do all kind of things; learning to fall in love might be easy." And it was what I really wanted to do. I wanted to experience falling in love.

One day he said: "Why do you wear such 'grandma' clothing with such a beautiful shape?" He said, "That dress you have on!" I can remember when I felt the same way about clothing that Christian women wore. He said, "I never want to see you in that again. Next week I'm going to take you shopping and buy you some clothing." Whenever we would go to the store he would disappear; what he would do is send me to get something in a different section of the store. He wanted me to wear tight-fitting clothing. So I did. He said, "I love the way you are built." I wanted to please him; whatever he bought for me was always fitting me tight; I wore whatever he wanted me to. When I would go down the different sections of the store he would watch other men watching me when I walked. I didn't know this until after we were married. He said, "I like to see other men watch you walk and when they approach you it makes me feel good that other men want to be with you."

I went to my girlfriend job again and I told her I was not sure he was the right person for me. She explained to me that there was nothing wrong with his asking me to dress a little sexier when I'm with him. She said, "You are just afraid of making a commitment with a decent guy. Look at this man's qualifications—he could have any woman he wanted. I am not trying to hurt your feelings, Gloria, but he has come down to the bottom of the barrel and he has chosen you. You are lucky that 'God' (*Elohim*) has blessed you with a man with such high standards; any woman would be lucky to have him." I begin to cry and I was thinking: "Am I really lucky am I the bottom of the barrel? I thought I was blessed." Something should have gone off in my head; I was letting her belittle me. All I wanted was to be accepted. Maybe I needed someone to justify what he was doing to me by making me feel bad about my godly decisions in come in agreement with his worldly desires. My girlfriend was making me feel like's I was trash in it was a privilege that he sought someone as low as me. I listened to what she was saying to me and I accepted her insults. Instead of stopping her I welcomed her spirit of criticism and I felt self-pity for myself; it came in and went to work on me. I began to tell myself "she's right," even though I knew she was not I could feel that feeling of hatred for myself again. She wasn't the problem, I was. I was allowing 'Bob' to disrespect me and my girlfriend to confirm it so that I can reinforce his bad behavior just as Adam did with Eve. I told myself, "do whatever he says and you will have a husband." It was a subtle deception from the halls of hell. A demon had found a place and a body to dwell in, and just like Adam I accepted what I knew was wrong. So many times we women accept what we know is not from the 'Holy Spirit' of "**Father Yah'uah**." I laid down what was right to do and accepted what was wrong.

It was almost time for 'Papa' Curt and his wife Gretchen to come for a visit. I had told them a little bit about what was going on in my life with Bob. I was secretive about most of the things that were going on between 'Bob' and me. I told 'Papa' Curt about his not being intimate with me. I was not telling the whole truth, I did not tell them about the feelings I was having about other women and of the marriage he had been involved with. I continued to see and feel the presence of other women whenever he was around me if he held my hand or touch me sometimes their 'presence' would be so strong that I would jump when the images would appear before me. I was seeing whole scene what had gone on between him and other women whenever he came near me. He would walk into the room and I would see a 'lady' walk into the room with him. By the time he would stand next to me. I would see at least a dozen women. I would see the entire outfit. They would have on these were, Physical images I was seeing one day when I was visiting him. He left a suitcase open and all the women that I was seeing their were pictures of them in that suitcase women that was doing all kinds of sexual acts in sexual poses. So I went back to my girlfriend the very next day I came home; she kept assuring me it was just my imagination and those with pictures of old girlfriends. Most people called me a 'prophetess;' that's the name Christian people gave me. For my entire life I had seen things that I could not explain to other people, and the things that I saw was —people, places— that would actually happen. I don't know why as a child I thought everybody saw these kinds of things. Sometimes I can't distinguish if what I'm seeing is real until I try to touch it, and then it will disappear. I explained to 'Bob' that I had that ability.

When I first met him 'Bob' had set a date for us to be married. He had bought me a ring early in our relationship; it was my engagement ring. When he and 'Papa' Curt met the conversation started out casual, but then 'Papa' Curt begin to minister to him. You could really see the face of evil on 'Bob;' he did not want to talk about any of his affairs with other women or how many times he had been married. He said 'Papa' Curt was invading his privacy, and he did not have the right to do so. We left the room, and he said to me: "Either you marry me now or not," so I asked 'Papa' Curt and his wife if they thought I should. They said they thought we should wait a little longer before making a decision, but 'Bob' was saying "right now, today." We had already gone a couple of days earlier and picked up a marriage license.

Once more I explained everything to my girlfriend and she said: "Look, everything you do with this man you feel like it is sin, and you do not have to tell 'Papa' Curt and his wife everything you do. Why do you feel the need to?" I said to her: "I feel that they are my real parents, and I want them to be proud of me." She said: "You are a grown lady." She said, "'God' wanted you to be married and to be happy with 'Bob.' You can't live your life by 'Papa' Curt and his wife. Stand up, be a woman and married that man." I knew once again I was listening to the voice of the enemy coming out of my girlfriend, who is a Christian, but at the time I wanted to be blind so I could be married. Yet I felt that I also knew the truth. I had my 'dad', 'Papa' Curt, and my 'mother' showing me the truth, and all I wanted was a lie. I just needed one person to reinforce what I wanted to do at the time. So my girlfriend became the mouthpiece I needed, even though I knew it was wrong. I just thought I needed a husband and I would do whatever it took to have one. I decided I would embrace sin, and all I needed was just one person to come in agreement with me. Then I could do what I knew was wrong, and my Christian girlfriend gave me her full support.

I said "yes" to 'Bob,' and so the next day I asked 'Papa' Curt if he would go someplace with us to do some ministry. I told him it was at a courthouse and the person really needed our help. I made up other lies about the person on our drive to the courthouse. Just like a good father, 'Papa' Curt came with us, thinking we were going to do some type of ministry. He knew that I would go almost anywhere and minister to people who needed it. He had been out 'on the street' with me on different occasions. He thought this was just another occasion where we would be helping someone.

When we got up to the courthouse we sat down and waited for our names to be called. Then I handed the lady the license. I had in an envelope. That's when 'Papa' Curt knew that we were going to be married that very day, and that he was about to be an unwilling witness to all of my madness and my insane behavior. It was an indication that I had set aside my only protection through *"Yah'shua"* the Messiah. I had rejected *"Yah'shua"* the Messiah so I could do what pleased my flesh. I had kidnapped 'Papa' Curt by lying to him. He tried to talk me out of my insanity but I wanted to do what my flesh decided. I wanted to do my own thing and I did not want to hear anything from anybody into wiping out the plans that **"Father Yah'uah"** had for me. I was lying and being very deceptive about everything concerning this man not only to Papa Curt and his wife, but to myself. I was embracing myself in the great deceiver giving up all of my birth right. That the Father Yah'uah had promised me, He uses everything and anything to destroy the plans of **"Father Yah'uah for me.**" It was me who make the final decision to give him what he wants. I read in the Bible, in Matthew 16:22–27: Then Peter took Him aside and began to rebuke Him, saying, "Far be it from you, 'Lord;' this shall not happen to you!" But He turned and said to Peter, "Get behind me, Satan! You are an offense to me, for you are not mindful of the things of 'God,' but the things of men." Then 'Jesus' said to His disciples, "If anyone desires to come after me, let him deny himself, and take up his 'cross' [stake], and follow me. For whoever desires to save his life will lose it, but whoever loses his life for my sake will find it. For what profit is it to a man if he gains the whole world, and loses his own soul? Or what will a man give in exchange for his soul? For the Son of Man will come in the glory of his Father with His angels, and then he will reward each according to his works." Also read Judges Chapters 14 through 16. If you read the whole Samson story you will see it in a different light. Delilah was not the first woman to deceive Samson; his wife also deceived him, I except 'Bob, my husband to be who was handpicked by Satan for me.'

If you look at this situation clearly you can see all of the characteristics of Satan deceiving me, a believer, when it comes to our flesh we give in most of the time.

After the marriage I began to have seizures again, because I was seeing so many different things. I had to dress like a call girl and dance in skimpy nightgowns for my husband. When I talked about it to my girlfriend she said we were married, and it was okay. I found myself always angry, always aggressive. Eventually the sexual acts got worse and worse. It got to where more and more I seemed to be losing control. I was having more frequent seizures, and especially when I would talk to him and when I acted in an ugly manner. I knew I was enraged, and it was just a matter of time before I would act it out. I could feel it coming and I did not know how to stop it. We got into such a bad argument one night because I did not want to perform a certain act. He also discussed with me about going to a nude beach. What had I gotten myself into? Was this the same man who said he loved "*Yah'shua*?" I had all the warning signs, but I refused to look at it for what it was. All I wanted was a husband and I thought this was the right man for me. When I myself clearly knew he was not. I had closed my eyes to all the warning signs; I would not accept the counsel of the 'Holy Spirit' that **"Father Yah'uah provided for me through Papa Curt and his wife**." Flesh will kill you dead if you continue following it, it has no morals for anyone regardless if you're young or old.

One day we were driving in the car. He insisted on me wearing a miniskirt, and he wanted me to remove my underwear so he could fondle me while he drove the car. That was it—I refused. Then the torture of fussing with me began. I was told, "You are not a good wife. Everything I want you to do you say "No." You don't please me, and you won't try anything different or new ways of making your husband happy. Maybe I have married the wrong woman. You have done all of this before in your life, so what's the big deal?" He was slapping me in my face with my past in order for me to perform in everything that was against Father

Yah'uah was well for me. He wanted to make sexual videos and go to nude beaches. I could not believe that a sixty-nine year's old man wanted a wife for that reason.

After he brought me back to Georgia he wanted to give me time to think about whether I was going to submit to what he wanted are not. Once again in my dilemma I went to my girlfriend at her job to talk to her. I told her about the dancing. She said: "I told you there's nothing wrong with that; it's just between you and your husband." I told her about him wanting me to dress up in different lingerie and dance for him. I told her I had done it and I felt so unclean, plus he had a camera and he wanted pictures. One night I woke up out of a sleep in a woman was there and the room with me, showing me where the camera was hidden in the bedroom. And then she just disappeared. He had taped the camera's legs with silver electrical tape. I was furious when I confronted him about the camera. He said, "No one will ever see this" and "this is for his private use only." I asked him to destroy the video. I know he pulled some of the tape out but I don't know how long he had been taping me.

He wanted to be with me sexually and I told him he would have to give me something to drink. I needed some type of alcohol. At that point I knew I was in trouble. I couldn't go back to my girlfriend, because she justified everything that was going on. She made me feel like everything he wanted to do was normal and I was the troublemaker. I had to think for myself. When things upset me I get extremely quiet; that quietness means it's 'fire in the hole' [a warning that indicates an explosive detonation in a confined space is imminent]. Anything could happen. I found myself praying in my head. I wasn't seeing things through the eyes of a child. I was asking "**Father Yah'uah**" to forgive me and help me out of this mess that I personally got myself into. I turned straight to the Messiah "*Yah'shua*." I kept repeating over and over in my head, "Please,"*Yah'shua*," do not let me do anything to harm another person." A peace came over me and I fell asleep.

That morning 'Bob' prepared breakfast for the two of us. I spoke to him very politely and very gently. He began to talk. He said he would buy me a house or give me the one we were in. He just wanted me to do one thing for him. He said, "You may choose any man you wanted to be with. All you have to do is let me watch." I knew at that moment what I was going to do; I asked him if he'd take me back to Geneva's house. So I could talk to the man. I would like to have sex when we arrived there at Geneva's house. He removed all of my things out of the car. When he got out of the car I said, "No, I don't want you to stay tonight." That was on a Sunday night. That Monday morning I drove to Richmond Hill to a little plaza with office buildings. There was a sign there which said, divorce for ninety-nine dollars. The paralegal there filled out the paperwork and sent a copy to 'Bob.' But 'Bob' would not fill out the paperwork or return his calls, so the paralegal had to use his cell phone instead of his business phone. 'Bob' answered the phone and the paralegal identified himself and asked 'Bob' if he would sign the paper work; he said, "Yes." But he would not. We had been married on January 30, 2006; all of this happened around March 5. 'Bob' did not sign the paperwork until June 24; our divorce was final on July 6.

More on 'Dissociative' Disorder

But I had other struggles and other things that "**Father Yah'uah**" was cleansing me of by writing this book. I said at the beginning of this book I was diagnosed with 'dissociative' disorder, and I thought that was because I separated myself from any type of pain I might feel. But while I was writing this book I would find places that I did not know how the sentiments got there. I did not realize that I was not alone in telling this story. So I talked to my daughter, and this is what she said to me: "When we were little you would say we could go outside. Then you would come looking for us and say, 'Who told you that you could go outside?'" I thought my children were making it up so that they could go outside, but now and only now do I see they were telling the truth. Now, through my writing, I see and remember things that I could not really remember before. I could not see the difference in my character. When I write it is like a bunch of people writing at the same time, trying to tell the same story. So I have to go in and fix this story, and because of that I am able to remember something that I had forgotten. I used to wonder how I could read one day and the next day I could not, why would I be doing 50 things at one time. The only thing that I am able to concentrate fully on is when I am taking care of people, figuring out ways to keep them from hurting. I really could not see all of the many unique characteristics of the real me. I have one goal and that is to stop the abuse at any cost, even though I have been the one who lashed out.

How I Lost My Shop

I am going to tell you now how I lost my shop. For about a year I had been praying with a lady named Pam whom I had met at a conference. She was going through a divorce, and it was tearing her apart. She wanted someone to pray with her and wanted **"Father Yah'uah"** to heal her marriage; she wanted counseling for herself and her husband and children. She so desperately wanted her marriage to work. So every day for almost a year we prayed.

One day Pam brought some things into my shop and then left. My landlady (and another woman) came in afterward and asked me about Pam. She wanted to know if I knew if Pam had a boyfriend. She warned me not to let Pam know she had asked about her, otherwise she would kick me out of my shop.

My landlord was trying to help Pam's husband take her children from Pam; they thought she should not have them. The next time I spoke to Pam I warned her not to go to any place that was not proper to be that people was watching her. I struggle two months because I did not want to tell Pam what had happened with my landlord eventually because my landlord told me she would put me out if my building if I did. I asked her not to mention it to her attorneys, and not to association with me or with 'The Heart of Christ, Inc.' I told her that my landlord said if I did, she would put me out of the building.

But it all came out in court. Pam had revealed to her attorney, and then to the judge, that she knew the landlady had asked me about her. However the landlady was true to her word and ended my lease. I'm not mad at Pam; if I were trying to keep my kids I would've done the same thing. I'm not mad at my landlady because she had done a lot of nice things for me, at least until that day.

Margaret's Perspective

I talked to Margaret recently and I asked her a whole lot of questions that I needed answers for. I asked her if she knew I was crazy. She said to me that she knew something was wrong, but she didn't think I was crazy. She said, "Everybody loves you, Gloria. You made sure people's children had food to eat. You gave people places to live. You helped them get their children out of jail. You made sure children started in school. When parents would put their children out you would take them in. Everybody loves you. And the way I've seen you take care of animals and especially babies! You would not turn those parents away. You took care of those other children like they were your own. And how even the animals love you! How could I not love you?" I said to her, "What about all of the stabbings and my fighting with you, and throwing hot water on you, or just screaming and crying for hours until I would literally fall asleep, sometimes not remembering any of it at all, or not remembering it even happened? Or I would accuse you of doing things to me. Or I would wake up crying and not know why? You were not able to tell me why I was crying and destroying the whole house. At what point did you think something was wrong with me?" She said, "I would watch you sit and literally work out problems for people. I knew that you would have to be someone who studied for a long time to know how to fix the problems. I would wonder sometimes how you would convince a mother to let her daughter or son go to a college, or not to pull her children out of school so that they could work and help take care of their family. You would help them until that child graduated from school. You are everybody's hero including mine."

I said I wanted to know, "At what point did you fear for your life?" She replied that she always did, but she knew I loved my children and "somebody had to take care of them to save them from you, when you got angry with them. When you'd go into a rage, at those times, no matter who was in your path, it made trouble. You tried your very best not to hit them and I know that. It was the children and I that made you leave the house so much; I just did not understand why. If anyone tried to stop you from hitting them it was worse for that person, and I was that person." She said, "I would watch you beat them and then go into depression, so somebody had to protect the children as well as you, Gloria."

"You gave your children so much stuff. You gave those children everything they wanted, and you would always find a way to get it for them if I would not give it to you. They had all kinds of stuff. You told them you loved them with every other word you used when talking to them. But you'd get angry if they told you a lie or stole something; you would go into a rage. You would not let them stay in anyone's house or spend a night out, not even with your friends. You were afraid for them to be around certain men or persons who you thought might be a threat to them. You would say, 'Stay in front of the window' where they were supposed to be playing. You told them they could play outside but to stay by the window so you could see them. Sometimes you could not remember something you told them to do; that's when they got in trouble. At school you totally went out of control! You wanted them to be able to read and write; school was the most important thing to you. You wanted something better for them than what you had. When you beat them I knew that you would not be back for months; I knew the toll it was taking on you. I stayed because I loved you and you needed someone to help you with your children. Besides that you were a good mother, and you were very good to people. I came into your life because you took me in off the street. You were for everybody, no matter what their color was or who they were. Even the police in New York loved you! I wish I could have stopped you from hurting, but you wouldn't tell me what was wrong. I know now that you did not know what was wrong with you. Gloria, you've come a long way. You were always trying to change somebody's life so they could be better, and I know you were trying to figure this whole thing out. The only thing you knew was you could not do it by yourself. I'm proud of you. You turned to the only One who could help you; it was your 'God.'"

I will always love Margaret. I am not talking about her in a sexual way, I'm talking about the way she helped me help people and for what she has done for my children and me. I pray for her all the time, asking **"Father Yah'uah"** to help her find "*Yah'shu*a." In His time I believe He will.

Nell and Her Family

I pray with a lot of people over the phone. I try my very best not to get connected to them. I tell myself, "I'm only there in their lives to strengthen them and give them the courage to stand with "**Father Yah'uah**" and to teach them the love that "*Yah'shua*" has for them."

I met Nell because I dialed the wrong number. I thought she was a white lady because she was so bubbly and happy to be alive. I said to her, "I have dialed the wrong number," but she said, "Okay, maybe I can help you." She helped me with what I was looking for and then she said, "Well I guess I'll say goodbye." So I said to her, "Can I pray for you?" and she replied, "Sure you can." We prayed and I told her what I heard "**Father Yah'uah**" say for her, and then she asked me if she could give my number to one of her sisters. That's how I met April. April reminds me of myself; she is determined to help everybody who comes into her life. She is a very strong-minded person and she is very bossy, but she's really a baby and she showers you with love. Her faith in *Elohim* is unshakable; she believes in her heart that she can move every mountain that gets in her way. After that I continued to meet most of Nell's brothers and sisters.

I had the privilege of meeting Nell's eighty-five-year-old father. He came with his daughter so I could pray for him. A couple of days after meeting him he wound up in the hospital. Blood was on his brain from a fall he'd had earlier; he could not move his hand and leg very well.

His daughters and son rushed their father to the hospital. He had to have emergency surgery. The family began to pray, and when they began to pray a miracle began to happen. After he came out of surgery and as soon as he opened his eyes it was as if nothing had happened to him at all. He had no slurring of his words, and his leg and hand worked perfectly. His family is so strange to me, because they have so much love and they are just giving it away. They have 'adopted' me into their family. You would think I had known them all of my life, yet I have not known them for even half of my life. But in the name of "*Yah'shua*" "**Father Yah'uah**" can put you in the family that will love you the most. As I said, He had given me back my brothers and sisters, cousins and uncles, nieces and nephews, and so many children. I'm in the largest family in the world. I read in my Bible, "In My Father's houses are many mansions; if it were not so, I would have told you."(John 14: 2).

Life in 'Christ'

It's been a long and rugged road. Sometimes "*Yah'shua*" has had to drag me all of the way, sometimes he has had to go get me out of nightclubs. Sometimes he has had to sober me up and wake me up. He has had to dress me and has had to wait for me to catch up. He has had to wash me and has had to hold me up through the loving kindness of all of His people, regardless of race. Father Yah'uah has given me my own father and mother by 'adopted' parents, who love me the Wagners. Father Yah'uah had to amend my relationship with my own daughter, Monique, as well as allow Sheila and Evelyn Byrd and so many other 'daughters.' To Love me and has fix things between my son and I Lesroy as well as Rice and Ben (son of the Wagners) and so many other 'sons.' There have been my nephews Kincade Douglas and all of my other nephews and nieces as well as my brothers and sisters in the name of "*Yah'shua*".

Before, I was trying to be a Christian for all of the wrong reasons. One of the reasons was so people would love me. The other reasons were so that I would fit in and no one would know my dirty little secrets. I was trying to be what people wanted me to be, not what "**Father Yah'uah**" *Elohim* called me to be. Then I was trying so it would be said, "Look, she's one of us. She is a Christian today." Now I am not trying to be the person that I was not called to be or pretending to be what I am not. I am who I am because of what "*Yah'shua*" did for me on the cross (stake,) because he was willing to do what his Father "**Yah'uah**" *Elohim* has really brought him into this world to accomplish in the name of "*Yah'shua*". All I want is to be like my "**Father Yah'uah**," my *Elohim*. I want to faithfully represent his only-begotten Son "*Yah'shua*," whose blood is my 'lathering soap.'

YAH Gives a Second Chance Ministry'

I want to tell you now about another miracle a vision I saw. I knew for about 10 years "**Father Yah'uah**" would put me in a house and I would take care of people in that house, and He would give me furniture. He did exactly that. Every stick of furniture in this house has been given to me. Some of it has come from friends and strangers, some from off the street, some out of fires, some off of the side of the road, some from ministries and some from schools, some from the military, and it all makes up this home. There is a wall covered with pictures. There is art throughout the house. There is a blue room with a blue floor. There is a purple room with a purple floor. The dining room is two-tone wintergreen with a soft mint green on the wall with white trimming, and the floor is green. In the kitchen and in the living rooms the walls are beige with brown wood trimming; the floors are beige, and white. And then there is the 'sanctuary:' its walls are gold with a yellow floor. The whole house is filled and surrounded by love.

Pam McCumberbatch had the floors put in for me. I had a young man come in and help me remove all of the carpets in the house. I am allergic to the outside and just about every kind of animal that walks around out there so I knew I could not have carpet. Even when I take care of animals my skin breaks out with sores, so the floor was filthy. So everything had to be pulled up. We did not have the money to cover the floor. After the young man removed the carpet there were nails coming out of the floors throughout the whole house. I was told by a carpenter that it would cost me $2500 for him to remove the nails. So I prayed about it and asked "**Father Yah'uah**" what to do. That small still 'voice' that I hear in my head I now recognize is the (Holy) Spirit of "**Father Yah'uah**" telling me what I need to do. I did not have anything to work with or any tool to wedge them out. So I got a hammer and a fork, and I got down on the floor in my underwear and began pulling up nails. Pam had a key to the house, so when she came in and saw me on the floor pulling up nails, she asked me, "What are you doing down there in your underwear, pulling up nails?" I explained to her that I had to take the nails out of the floor. She looked at me with a beautiful smile on her face and said, "Pastor, get off the floor, you have no business being down there like that." I told her I didn't know any other way to get the nails out of the floor. So Pam began to laugh at me. She said, "You should be doing other things." Then she asked, "What are you going to put down there?" I said, "We simply don't have the money to put anything down there yet." So she said, "Pastor, please put on some clothes and we will go and find some coverings for the floor." Consequently Pam and her sister Ann and I went looking everywhere in Glennville, Georgia, but everything was too expensive. So we had lunch and stopped looking. The next day I heard the 'voice' within my head saying, "Go to Hinesville; go down 196; turn on 84." That is what I did. That is where I stopped driving. I drove the car a little further down the street and that is where I saw this place that sold all types of floor coverings. I walked in and asked the man if I could call Pam so she could tell him what I needed. I knew what I needed but as soon as I walked in the door the 'voice' said, "Call Pam." I handed my phone to the man; he and Pam talked for awhile.

Then he asked me to show him what I needed, and there it was—the tile that "Father Yah'uah" had told me to buy. All the colors were there at that place—the blue, beige, green, purple, and gold. So Pam and her sister Ann took care of the flooring for this house.

I want to take you back in time. After we had purchased the land, Pastor Mickey Jackson paid to have a septic tank put in, and 'Papa' Curt and friends of mine paid to have a deep well put in. I was originally from New York City but raised, up in Brooklyn, New York. I had never seen those types of things. I didn't really know they existed until I came to Georgia. So I had to find someone to put them in for me at that time. The 'voice' in my head continued telling me to put those things in even though we did not yet have any house or trailer. So I thought, "If we do not have a house or a trailer what do we need them for?" After a year had passed there was still no house or trailer. So I talked to Gloria Brown about it. She was the lady I wanted to run 'The Heart of Christ, Inc.' and take care of all the paperwork and apply for grants. We needed Gloria so badly to take care of that part of 'The Heart of Christ, Inc.' One day she just walked in to 'The Heart of Christ, Inc.' building and offered her services. She did all she could to help me. If it had not been for Gloria Brown giving us a large donation, the Ministry would have closed, and I am so grateful to her for that. She also has a very good heart for people. However we had a lot of differences on how we wanted the Ministry to be run and that caused us conflict.

I wanted people to feel that they were not being judged and that each person's problem was important to us. I have had lots of people come and try to bully me. But when I would talk to them as though I knew where they were coming from they would back down. They realized I knew exactly what their problems were and the limitations of their finances. All they really wanted was to ensure that their family would be taken care of. Yes, some of them were drug users, but I had learned how to recognize them immediately because I had lived with one the first part of my life and Mama was the best at manipulating the system. So when I had to deal with a client with that type of attitude I knew how to bring them to the real world. Also it gave me a chance to minister the love of 'Jesus Christ' and the 'Holy Spirit.' I would say I am not the one taking care of them and it was not the system, it was 'God' (**"Father Yah'uah"** *Elohim*) through his people. I was only representing them. I explained to them how He brought them to this point in their lives, so that He could have people there representing Him, and they would be able to see that He had not forgotten them. He was there waiting for them. We were only the bodies and hands waiting to do whatever **"Father Yah'uah"** wanted us to do. We were the ones representing the people whom **"Father Yah'uah"** had chosen to provide the things they needed. It was **"Father Yah'uah"** doing it for them because He loved them. He did not want them to make the mistake of believing that I or anyone else was doing it for them. The whole outlook of that person would change because they knew at that very moment that God **"Father Yah'uah"** *Elohim* truly loved them and their families, no matter, who they were or who had rejected them for the first time they were hearing and seeing the love of **"Father Yah'uah"** *Elohim* in action. I wanted each person to know that it was **"Father Yah'uah"** who had helped them. Any person who is going through something hard feels intimidated, and I did not want them to feel that way. There was always some paperwork that had to be done, but the way we talked to people made all the difference even when they are being nasty to us. I told Gloria Brown I kept hearing the inner 'voice' telling me to go ahead and put in the septic tank and deep well, and "**Father Yah'uah**" would do the rest. She said to me, "Gloria, you've had that land for over a year. Go ahead and listen to what 'God' ("**Yah'uah**" *Elohim*) is telling you to do." So I got a telephone book and I started calling around. I finally found a company that would put in the deep well, and they knew a company that would put in the septic tank. It was around the eighth or ninth of December, I think, when the men came out with big trucks and all kinds of heavy-duty equipment. They asked me where I wanted the septic tank to go. I said, "In the back," but they put it to the side, and the deep well they put in the front yard. I did not know where they were really supposed to go. I just knew that the septic tank went into the ground first and then the deep well.

I'm going to give you a description of what the men were doing. It was about seven o'clock in the morning when they got here. Some of them were drinking beer and some were drinking whiskey straight out of the bottles. They were talking to one another while they were working. A 'voice' in my head said, "Look." So I did, and the water was gushing up from the hole in the ground. It was so clear and sparkling; I had never seen anything like that before. I stepped out of the car and began to walk toward the well where the men were working. When I looked up butterflies appeared out of nowhere; they were yellow with brown spots on their wings. They did not fly in, they just appeared there!

Everybody was stunned as we watched the butterflies appear; more and more of them kept appearing. Then they started flying towards me. I started screaming and waving my hands to try and shoo them away while running to my car. Before I even got to the car I was completely surrounded by many butterflies. Then when I did get to the car I had to fumble with the door until I finally got the car door open. The butterflies should have flown into the car, but they didn't. Not one of them flew in. They hovered by my window for a few moments and then they just disappeared. The man who owned the deep well company said he had done this work for about forty-something years. He had never seen that type of butterfly in December. He and his crew began to pour out their liquor and beer onto the ground. One of the men said he was going through a divorce. He asked me if I would pray with him. He was on his knees with his hands stretched out. He asked 'God' ("**Father Yah'uah**" *Elohim*) in the name of 'Jesus' ("*Yah'shua*") if he could forgive him for his sins and save his marriage that day. Those men asked me to lead them to 'Jesus Christ' ("*Yah'shua*" the Messiah) right then and there! There had to be at least 13 or 14 men on the property and they wanted to be led to 'Jesus' ("*Yah'shua*"). That was one of many miracles that have happened on this property. I have seen people come with all sorts of ailments, going through divorces, having cancer in the body, afraid of going to jail. No matter what sort of problem they were having they said that 'Jesus' ("*Yah'shua*") had brought about some type of change in them. I also saw people who would belittle me or come against me for no reason; some would call me a wicked witch. "**Father Yah'uah**" would deal with them and I did not have to do anything to them. The word of "**Father Yah'uah**" says it in 1

Chronicles 16:21–22: "He permitted no man to do them wrong; Yes, He rebuked kings for their sakes, Saying, 'Do not touch my anointed ones, and do my prophets no harm.'"

My Name of 'Christ'

A lot of times people will ask me, "Did you change your name to Christ, because you think you are a 'god' or that you are 'Jesus Christ'?" When I tell them, "Certainly not," they don't believe me. I changed my name because I did not know what my family name really was at that time. I had become a Christian, and I had a whole big family. I had heard 'God' (*Elohim*) tell me to change my last name to 'Christ.' 'Christ' is not a last name of 'Jesus' "*Yah'shua*." The English word 'Christ' comes from a Greek word that means 'anointed.' It is used to describe anyone anointed with (olive) oil for any 'royal' service, for example in the Temple or the military or the government. It is the equivalent of the Hebrew word *mashiach* or the English word messiah. If you were called the 'Christ,' or the Messiah, that person would be saying, "You are an anointed one of 'God, Father Yah'uah'." Usually kings were anointed with (olive) oil when they were called to be kings. King David when still a boy was anointed with oil by Samuel. After "**Father Yah'uah**" had set him apart, David said to King Saul: "The LORD [i.e. "**Yah'uah**"] forbid that I should do this thing to my master, the LORD's anointed *(mashiach)*, to stretch out my hand against him, seeing he is the anointed *(mashiach)* of the LORD" (1 Samuel 24:6). So the title of messiah or 'Christ' acknowledges 'an anointed one,' meaning that the anointed person is now set apart to do a special job for "**Father Yah'uah**." So when we hear "Do not touch my anointed ones, and do my prophets no harm" (1 Chronicles 16:22), it means "**Father Yah'uah**" protects us in the things He has asked us to do. In

Genesis 12:10–17, Abraham had an anointing on his life because of his assignment by **"Father Yah'uah."** **"Father Yah'uah"** had given him the anointing to do the job plus the faith he needed to believe **"Father Yah'uah."**

I know I am not an intelligent woman, not because I do not try to learn things, but because Satan our enemy issued an assignment against me from the earliest days of my life. However it was **"Father Yah'uah,"** through the shed blood of His only-begotten Son, *"Yah'shua"* the Messiah, Who set me free! For a part of his service, not because I wanted to do it because he knew through all of my faults I would be faithful in doing them. Now His name means everything to me. I hope that in the reading of this book it will help my son know who his mother really is and he will find a way to ask **"Father Yah'uah"** to help him forgive me so he can heal.

My Condition Apart From 'God'

The way I see myself when I see myself through the eyes of a child "**Father Yah'uah**" *Elohim* is that I am wandering hopelessly through a hazy maze and there's no one to help me get on track, or I'm drowning in filth, like being in sewer water. I feel like I'm unable to climb out. I wish that I could find the strength to take my first step, but I can't. I keep going backward, over and over again. If only I could find a friend who could help me out of my dilemma by just lending me a hand. I am not really a loving person; I am only hateful. I am unkind and unlikable, and I'm unthankful, unloving, and unfriendly. If only I could just touch one of the hands of "*Yah'shua*," maybe only the fingertips, he would see me and save me from drowning in this filthy hellhole in which I now find myself. I know a touch from his fingertips would wash me clean. No more would I be groping in the shadows of death and wondering in the world of the belly of hell, "Is my *Elohim* going to come and save me?" I would at last be set free from the curses (from family sins) that have been handed down to me from generation after generation of my family—both from my father's and my mother's sides of the family. I would at last be cleansed from all of the sins in misery against me that I have committed—both willingly and unwillingly against me. [The TaNaKh ('Old Testament') in several places refers to the sins of the fathers affecting succeeding generations, e.g. in the second commandment in Exodus 20:5–6 "you shall not bow down to them nor serve them. For I, 'the LORD' [" **Father Yah'uah**"] your 'God,' [*Elohim*] am a jealous 'God,' visiting the iniquity of the fathers upon the children to the third and fourth generations of those who hate Me, but showing mercy to thousands, to those who love Me and keep My commandments." This is the basis for 'family curses' [openings for demonic attacks on family members] to be passed down through unrepentant generations. Of course each of us is accountable also to 'God' Father Yah'uah for our individually, as written in Deuteronomy 24:16 "Fathers shall not be put to death for their children, nor shall children be put to death for their fathers; a person shall be put to death for his own sin" whatever goes on in the household and a child is raised in the child will have those characteristics somewhere in their lives.

If only I could see myself clean. I'd been told that there is a way that I could be cleansed from all of my sins. I thought, "How could that be?" My friend said I would be cleansed as though I had used lathering soap. She said all I would have to do is accept 'Jesus' ("*Yah'shua*") into my heart and call on the name of 'Jesus' ("*Yah'shua*"), and the name alone would cleanse me. How could that possibly be? Wouldn't he have to touch me or bathe me?" My friend said, "No! " He would bathe me in his shed blood and would cleanse me with his love. He would fill me with the Spirit of "**Father Yah'uah**" his Father, and that same Spirit would teach me and lead me into all truth "**Father Yah'uah**" *Elohim* would be revealed to me in so many different ways. He would be my strength in times of trouble. He would be my friend when there were none. I would never be alone because He would always be there. If I were sad He would give me joy; He would turn my sadness into true happiness. If

I had lost everything He would help me replace it all. If I were poor or out of work, He would provide for my needs. If I desired to marry he would find me a husband. If I couldn't have children He would surround me with many children who needed my love. He would also give me children to call my own, children who have been forgotten and left alone with no one to love them or care for them. He would give me an abundance of love for them in order to help lead them into His Kingdom, and He will love them Himself.

Yes, the Spirit of "**Father Yah'uah**" *Elohim* will always be there for you. He is the only One who can lead you over the rough roads that you are walking on. So seek "*Yah'shua*" the Son who will point you to his Father, "**Yah'uah**" *Elohim*. He will bring you into the Kingdom of Glory to be in the Holy Presence of the King of the Universe, "**Father Yah'uah**" *Elohim*. It is His shield of Glory that reigns over and protects me. That is the way He sees me and that is the way he wants me to see myself in His Holy Glory. There is no shame or uncleanness, just His Glory and His Name. And so He has also given you a perfect name that has no shame in His eternal Kingdom.

Anticipating Glory

I have been born twice. I have died to myself because I have found myself in the eyesight of the Messiah "*Yah'shua*," the King of kings. He did not reject me. He did not treat me coldly. He did not allow me to think in the past, nor did He allow my soul to grow weary. He allowed me to see myself as the daughter I was meant to be in His eyes. I have been created in my Father's (spiritual) image. He doesn't see me as a female, and certainly not as a male. He sees me in His Glory and Essence. He sends His 'Holy Spirit' to find me when I'm in the darkest places. He sends His 'Holy Spirit' to guide me when I have lost my way. He sends His 'Holy Spirit' to teach me that I may have the wisdom of my Father "**Yah'uah**" *Elohim* for each and every day. Oh, how I long for the day when I will be perfectly whole and kneeling in the Presence of my Messiah "*Yah'shua*" and my Father "**Yah'uah**" *Elohim*. All of my hopes and all of my dreams have pointed me to the Throne of my Father. "**Yah'uah**" *Elohim* waits for me to stand before Him and in this very way He will be judging me fairly and true because He knew my heart before he created me. All of His glory and all of His wisdom will be there, reading from a great book that has been prepared for you and me. On every page you will see how many times He had to pardon me. You see, this book has been prepared especially for you and me. He will judge you and me because we are family and clearly he will judge you and me so that all will see the fairness in the righteousness of my Father, the King, "**Yah'uah**" *Elohim*. He has guided me to this very day; for this very day I surrender, I surrender to my Father Yah'uah *Elohim*. I will give up my rights so I can stand with those who love Him in every way. Oh, how I wait to be in that number before Him and before His great love. Yes, Father "**Yah'uah**" I wait for that day…

I want to end my story with a blessing for you, dear reader. Whenever I call 'Papa' Curt I always ask him to say a particular blessing over me before we hang up. That is the 'Aaronic Blessing' that "**Father Yah'uah**" *Elohim* commanded Aaron and the Levitical priests to pronounce over the Hebrew Israelites so that He, "**Father Yah'uah**" Himself, would bless them. This way all credit and glory goes to "**Father Yah'uah**" *Elohim* and not to any man or woman. The blessing is found in the *Torah* in Numbers 6: 24–26 (KJV) as:

"*The* **LORD** *bless thee, and keep thee:*

The **LORD** *make His Face shine upon thee, and be gracious unto thee:*

The **LORD** *lift up His countenance upon thee, and give thee peace.*

Unfortunately, this KJV translation uses the *code* words 'The LORD' as a *substitution* for (and a *nullification* of) the actual given Name of our Creator [which *breaks* the third commandment!]. So when 'Papa' Curt pronounces this essential blessing over me, he always speaks it in the beautiful Hebrew tongue as recorded in the Hebrew Scriptures of the *Torah*. He does not follow the rabbinical tradition of substituting the title *Adonai* for the given Name of **YHWH**, but instead he pronounces His Hebrew Name (as best he knows how).

Here is his *literal* English translation of the 'Aaronic Blessing' using the Strong's numbers from Zodhiates' The Complete Word Study Old Testament (King James Version) with its Hebrew dictionary reprinted from Strong's Exhaustive Concordance of the Bible:

"**YAH'UAH** *bless you and do [put a protective] hedge [as with thorns] about you;*

YAH'UAH *make luminous His 'face' ('presence') to you and do bend [and stoop in kindness] to you;*

YAH'UAH *do lift His 'face' ('presence') to you and do put safety [in mind and body] to you."*

v.27: "*And they shall put* **My Name** *upon the sons of Israel, and* **I** [**Myself**] *will bless them!"*

[Scripture quotations are from the New King James Version, unless otherwise noted.]

Appendix: Divine Names and Titles

Some introductory explanations are necessary because the names and titles for Deity used in this testimony are not the usual KJV biblical words like 'Lord', 'LORD', 'God', 'GOD', etc. Even though many believers are content using those KJV English words as names, or lack reasons to search more deeply, the fact is that none of those words are actually true names of the Divine, but are mere titles, and ancient pagan ones at that! We should want to know the actual 'personal' Name(s) of the Creator so we can praise and pray to our Creator in a personal way. But the question of what is His Name is actually posed in the Scriptures themselves. Probably the best example is found in Prov.30: 1–9, particularly verse 4 which ask the reader "…what is His Name and what is the name of His son, if you know?" The author (not Solomon here) answers the first

Question in verse 9, but you won't see the actual Name unless you look at the verse in the Hebrew text! [Instead you will only see the English 'code words': 'the LORD'].

A much more familiar Scripture passage is Exodus 3: 1–15, which describes the famous 'burning bush' event in which 'Moses' is puzzled by the bush that appeared to be on fire but did not burn up! Then a messenger ['angel'] of the Creator spoke to 'Moses' out of the flames. Through this messenger the Creator tells 'Moses' that He has chosen him to lead the Israelites out of their bondage in Egypt. Knowing that the Israelites would be suspicious of any self-proclaimed liberator, 'Moses' asks how he should answer their likely (and legitimate) question of the Name of the 'God' sending and enabling him [verse 13]. Then the Creator (again through His 'angel') answers 'Moses' in verse 14 with His authoritative ('full') Name. When the Hebrew words are transliterated into English sounds the result would sound something like:

"ehyeh asher ehyeh."

Most English Bibles have something like 'I Am Who I Am', but most Hebrew scholars would admit that that is simply not correct. [An amplified version might be: 'I Am Who I Am; I Was Who I Was; I Have Been Who I Have Been; I Had Been Who I Had Been; I Will Be Who I Will Be; I Will Have Been Who I Will Have Been; …!']. In fact they might admit that the Hebrew expression can not be translated into English, or any language. It seems to have precise meaning <u>only</u> when spoken in the <u>Hebrew</u> tongue!

We do not attempt to use that 'full' Name here, but rather we use the 'personal' Name that the 'angel' (or messenger) of the Creator instructed 'Moses' to use [verse 15]. The Name revealed to 'Moses' was the four-Hebrew-letter combination that scholars call the Tetragrammaton—"**yud heh vav heh**" or "**yud heh waw heh.**" [This is the Name that appears in Prov.30: 9]. The equivalent four-Roman-letter combination for these Hebrew letters would be **YHVH** or **YHWH**. The exact way to pronounce these four Hebrew consonants has been lost over the millenia, but there are several theories. The most familiar or usual pronunciation today is probably '*Yahweh*' as it appears in the (Catholic) Jerusalem Bible. The version familiar to users of Strong's Exhaustive Concordance of the Bible is H3068 = '*Yehovah*' or '*Yehowah*' (or **YeHoVaH** or **YeHoWaH**) and represented as **YHVH** or **YHWH**. These various forms might be called the 'formal' or 'academic' Names.

In my own life I have known and used the Name of '*Yahweh*' ever since I was 'born again' in 1973. But as I slowly discovered more and more of my own 'Hebraic roots,' I had a deep desire to know my Creator more intimately by better knowing His Name. After several years of puzzling over the deeper meaning of the Hebrew text of Gen.2: 7 I believe that I am getting closer to 'knowing' His 'personal' Name and why in fact it is not even pronounceable! I now believe it can only be aspirated. However, an approximate way of trying to pronounce that aspiration would be "**Yah'uah**," which would be represented as **YHWH**. I use this 'personal' form in personal prayers and praises, or whenever His Name is actually spoken in the Scriptures. Whenever the Creator is only referred to, I often use His 'formal' or 'academic' Name, 'Yahweh' or '*Yehovah*'. His 'personal' Name, "**Yah'uah**," has been adopted in this autobiography.

For completeness we should add that there is a shorter, contracted form of His 'personal' Name "**Yah'uah**", what might be called His 'intimate' Name: "**Yah**" [or **YaH** and represented by **YH**]. This

Name should be familiar to most believers who say or sing or hear the English praise word "Hallelujah" (or "Alleluia"). Found in many of the Psalms, it is actually a compound Hebrew word "*Hal'lu*Yah" which means "Praise **Yah**!" Anyone who uses this 'intimate' Name should really have an 'intimate' relationship with "**Yah'uah**!" It was her discovery that a form of this Name ['Jah'] was actually in her KJV Bible in Psa.68: 4 that led Ms. Gloria Christ to incorporate that 'intimate' Name in her Georgia outreach ministry, '**YAH** Gives A Second Chance Ministry.'

The question of the Divine Title to be used for **YHVH** (or **YHWH**) is much simpler. There are three Hebrew words that English Bibles translate as 'God': *'el* [H410]; *'eloah* [H433]; and *'elohim* [H430], which is the plural of *'eloah*. When used as a title for a person the singular words should best be translated as '(a) mighty one.' The plural word should be translated as '(an) almighty one' for one person ['Moses' in Ex.7: 1], or 'mighty ones' for more than one person [Judges in Ps.82: 6, as alluded to by 'Jesus' in Jn.10: 34]. However when these Hebrew words are used as a <u>title for **YHVH** (or **YHWH**</u>) the singular words should be capitalized and be translated as '(The) Mighty One.' The plural word should be capitalized and translated as '(The) Almighty One.' This English form is used to indicate that this plural Hebrew grammar represents a plurality <u>not of Persons</u> but of Might, Power, and Sovereignty! This is consistent with the fact that this plural Hebrew noun always takes a singular Hebrew verb (i.e., it acts singularly, as <u>one</u>). In this autobiography the plural form of *Elohim* is always used, and it should be translated as '(The) Almighty One.'

Finally, we need to answer the second question in Prov.30: 4, which is 'what is the Son's name?' I can only answer this question from my own personal ('Damascus road') encounter with the Spirit of the Creator **YHWH**. The Spirit of **YHWH** directed me to call on 'Jesus' [a name with which I was familiar] through which name I was redirected back to the Creator Himself! But what is the Son's actual <u>Hebrew</u> name? From the Greek texts for Acts 7: 45 and Hebrews 4: 8 it is apparent that the author of Acts ['Luke'] and the unknown author of Hebrews [not 'Paul'] both used the same Greek word for 'Joshua' as they did for 'Jesus' [G2424]. Now the Hebrew word translated as 'Joshua' in most English Bibles is Strong's H3091, which is transliterated as '*Yehoshua*' and means '*Yehovah*-saved.' Thus in any 'formal' discussion or reading of the Son's name I use the name '*Yehoshua*', the 'only-begotten Son' of '*Yehovah*' [**YHVH**]. For personal praise or prayer in his name I use a corresponding vowel-pointing of H3091 which is transliterated as "*Yahushua*" and means "**Yah'uah**-saved". In that context I use the name of "*Yahushua*" for the 'only-begotten Son' of "**Yah'uah**" [**YHWH**]. If this 'personal' name is spoken quickly in prayer or praise it comes out sounding like "*Yah'shua*", and it is this version which is used in this autobiography. But in either form the Son's name points to and is derived from his and our Heavenly Father—"**Yah'uah**"—[**YHWH**]. So let everlasting praise and glory be to His Eternal Name!

Dr. Curt Wagner
Marshall, MN
14 Tevet 6011
(9 January 2012)

Contact

If any of my sisters or their children are still living, please contact me at P.O. Box 903, Hinesville, GA 31310. My sister named her oldest daughter is my name, Gloria Mae Stewart. Her other daughter's name is Ritchie Powell. My sister's name is Gail Christine Powell or Stewart. I've been looking for y'all. I have not stopped loving y'all. I am still working out different parts of my life, but I am doing it with family from the household of "Father **Yah'uah**" my *Elohim*.

Epilogue

Writing this book has not been easy, I have found. I cried a lot in some places, I laughed in some places, I said to myself "what was I thinking?" in other places. I thank *"Yah'shua" HaMashiach* ('Jesus the Christ') for his shed blood and for being the head of my life, and the 'Holy Spirit' of **"Yah'uah"** for making my Father **"Yah'uah"** real to me.

I have not turned my back on **"Yah'uah"** since that time when I first found Him, no matter what has happened. I know I have to stay under the protection of *"Yah'shua"*. It was a bittersweet road but I had to walk it, and in walking it I found myself. I embraced the 'Holy Spirit' because I made the choice to get out of an unhealthy relationship. I did not let any of the things of this world separate me from the love of *Elohim*. I had compromised my life for my children, I had compromised my life for their fathers, but this time I had to make a choice. I have a good 'father' and 'mother' who do not support divorce, but they stood by me in my decision making and to this day they still stand by me in my decision making.

After I finished writing this book I had a DNA Ancestry Test done in order to learn more about my possible ancestral heritage. I always have wondered why I felt such an unusual closeness to 'Jewish' people. But the results of the DNA Ancestry Test revealed one 'Jewish' I marker (in one of my parents). Most (5/9) of the markers were not surprisingly in 3 of the 4 Sub-Saharan African groups (II-IV). However there were 2 markers (in both parents) in Native American group II and one marker in Eastern European group II (which could also indicate possible 'Jewish' ancestry). Though these genetic markers do not reveal conclusive results, I now feel that I finally know more about who I am and why I think and act the way I do…

Acknowledgements

To Mr. and Mrs. Scott and Jessica Sorensen: When the Christian community made me an outcast you continued to show me love. Pastor Dacey Edwards: From the very beginning of my journey to finding my way to "*Yah'shua*" you were there. You would not let me get discouraged by the things that were said and done to me by my brothers and sisters. You continued to see the love of "Father **Yah'uah**" *Elohim* in me. And most of all to my nephew, Kincade Douglas: For always reminding me that I am a human being, and that "Father **Yah'uah**" has created me in His own image. Margaret Autry: for everything you've done for me and my children, and for helping me with other peoples' children and helping me change the lives of other adults and animals I was trying to rescue. Dr. Richard Anderson and Misty Young: you said to me, "You are not crazy. You just process things differently." Rob English: for all the help you've given me in Ministry and in my personal life. Mr. and Mrs. Rice and Mr. David and his wife from Youth Challenge: for all the time you were there when I needed the Youth Challenge to help me. Pastor Harmon Scott: for your encouraging words that I overheard—they have anchored and I will take them to my grave. My prayer partners Tara Anderson and Mackie Riley, and Charlie Price and Sylvia Jones: you've tried your very best to see that I stay healthy. Miss Inez Powell: who has accepted and loved me as a sister unconditionally, regardless of my past; you only see my future. Patricia Moore: you have always encouraged me to complete this book with every kind of help you could give me. I want to thank you Dr. Seth A. Borquaye, M.D., and my dentist Dr. J. and his wife.

Now to the citizens of Hinesville, thank you for helping me find myself and allowing me to be an ambassador for. The citizens of Hinesville, You have helped me realize that I am worth something in your eyes, that I am a real person with real feelings. I know I have not mentioned everybody here but you know what you have done in my life and the lives of others. May "Father **Yah'uah**" continue to let all of you be a blessing to others?

I also want to thank all of the following people and businesses who turned my life away from a living hell and who trusted me and have supported 'The Heart of Christ, Inc. ': Mr. Rob English; Mr. and Mrs. Robert and Lydia Clark for teaching me how to count money; my bank tellers at First Citizen's Bank and Coastal Bank, especially Ms. Brenda; every staff member at the post office especially Mr. Cesar Rodriguez, Mrs. Angelee Mitchell, Mrs. Ann Rife and Mr. Steve, (you have a big place in my heart for all the good things you have done); the soldiers and the chaplains from Fort Stewart who have lent a helping hand to our community; Youth Challenge (a preventive program for high school dropouts) who helped me clean until the day I left 'The Heart of Christ, Inc.' building; Mr. Gary Dodd who put my clients to work; the owner of Hinesville Ford, who has blessed many people; Mr. Poole's Deli for feeding my clients and for trusting me to pay when I got the money; The Western Sizzler which has helped feed so many of my clients and some of the staff who have given me money to put families up in a hotel; Sparkling Car

Wash which on numerous occasions helped me and collected pennies to help our community; Wal-Mart which has donated the very best of what they had so that I could repair broken items given to the ministry to give to the elderly and toys to children who were mentally handicapped, whose parents did not have a lot of money. I could go on and on without stopping about all the good things that the people of Hinesville, Georgia did for me in bringing about my education and healing, and helping me no longer see myself looking through the eyes of a child. There wouldn't be enough pages in this book to begin to acknowledge all the good things that the citizens of Hinesville, Georgia did for me in bringing about my education and healing, and for helping me to no longer see myself through the eyes of a child. Hinesville: you have been a community blessing the people who most needed help, and always working with one goal in mind—to bring change to someone's life. Finally, thanks to my 'adopted' father and mother, my 'Papa' Curt and 'Mama' Gretchen Wagner, for all the love, all the praise, all the patience, and all the prayers. You have given me the most of all!

I would also like to say thank you to Tim B. from Amazon.com. This book could not have been published without his help. I never learned his real name but his personality will leave an impact on me for the rest of my life. He did not look at my shortcomings, he just jumped in and poured a lot of patience understanding sympathy and love into helping me get this book out there. This man went far beyond just doing his job. He really took the time and patience to make sure my voice was heard. I understand how to use a computer with the help of Dragon Naturally Speaking but all the other things is like a foreign language to me. He did not ever look at my handicap or my lack of understanding he just found ways to help me and ways to build me up. The whole time he worked with me he would explain everything to me no matter how many times he had to do it and make sure I understood what we were doing. I told him I have a tendency to forget things, so he would send me notes or help me create documents to keep track of things. Mr. Tim. B never represented himself, always his company. He always acted so professional and polite. But in his actions I see not just a person who goes beyond the call of duty for his company and his customers but the making of a great man. Amazon.com has a lot of wonderful people working with the disabled, but no one like Mr. Tim B. He is totally a blessing from Father Yah'uah God, and I pray to Father Yah'uah God that I will get to meet Tim B. in person so I can thank him face-to-face.

Testimonials

"I would like to take this time to express what an impact that Mrs. Gloria Christ has had on me and my husband's lives. She is truly a person of 'God.' She has inspired us in so many ways. She has the 'Holy Spirit' dwelling within her and if you have ever been in contact with her your life will change forever and for the best. She is a very motivated person and always has time for others. She puts others' needs before her own, just as our Father 'God' gave His Son for our sins."

-Roger Rice Sr. and Sheila Rice

"I would like to take this time to share an amazing experience with you all about Sister Gloria Christ. She has been such an inspiration in my life. After a short time of meeting her, my husband was diagnosed with cancer and everything around me was falling apart. Sister Gloria Christ came in as if she had been sent as an angel in the time of need. Not only did she lift me up in mind, body, and spirit but she gave me hope and understanding. She also ministered to and comforted me as well as my 11 children. She is truly a person of 'God.' My husband needed round-the-clock care so therefore Sister Gloria Christ closed her business for 6 months to help give him care. She helped each of us grieve individually in our own way for the loss of their father and my husband. It is like the old saying "He is an on time 'God' all the time" and she is always on time. She is a very caring person and she was handpicked by 'God' to do his work."

-Mrs. Louise Grant

"When I first met Gloria, in April 1999, I sensed that she was a person through whom 'God' was at work. My family and I were stationed at Fort Stewart near Hinesville, Georgia, and I was enrolled in a course on counseling. As part of my school requirement I needed to meet and talk to people in the role of a 'student counselor.' At that point in time I was not finding and meeting and talking to enough 'counselees' in as many settings as I needed to complete my course. I thought that I might meet people who were in need of physical things like food and clothing, who would probably have need of someone to listen to their stories, and perhaps even need some advice and encouragement. I could write their stories (without their names, of course) and what kind of help I thought would be suitable for them, and complete my course.

I had read about 'The Heart of Christ, Inc.' (THOC) in the local newspaper—it might have been a promotional piece, or a story about the city of Hinesville taking her grant money, I don't remember. At any rate I dropped in at THOC in the course of some other errands in town. When Gloria greeted me she said: "Tell me what to do for you." [Normally service or salespeople ask "May I help you?" or "How may I help you? Not always with a genuine attitude of helpfulness.] When I told Gloria my situation, she might have been skeptical or cautious, and I was prepared to explain further or to be dismissed politely.

Instead she 'hired' me on the spot. "I have a man with cancer I want you to come talk to," as in, go to his house that very minute.

I wasn't prepared to make the visit that day but we set a time and date to visit the man. Hence I was back on track with my schoolwork, instead of having to drop the course or spend money for a more formal internship. I determined to contribute some time, work and occasionally funds to Gloria's work in return for her providing this opportunity. After all, when I completed my degree I stood to receive an increase in pay and become more competitive for promotion in my Army career.

Gloria introduced me to people in and around Hinesville and Glennville whom I would not have met in any other context. There were people of humble means, in large families, and even some afoul of the law. Because Gloria had established relationships with them they accepted me as someone they could speak with. Many were some of the loveliest people I remember ever meeting, and on a couple occasions I was served some of the best food I remember ever eating. At a rural church where I led a Bible study on Wednesday evenings (for the purpose of my course I called it 'adult literacy') on a couple occasions the pastor turned over their offering to me—a few dollars—for gas money. I have rarely been so honored or humbled. Along with a couple of my teenage children (for whom I thought it made for good experience) I helped the man with cancer (it was in remission) to reestablish his business in town for a time. I met others—business people or computer techies—who contributed what they could to Gloria's ministry, also lovely people.

Being accustomed to membership in large organizations, like the Army or church or my college, I thought it was important for Gloria to cooperate or 'partner' with other organizations like churches and helping agencies. This would provide some oversight, security, accountability, and so on, to THOC. After a couple of years of seeing attempted 'partnerships' come and go, it occurred to me that Gloria was not so much a 'priest' who is part of a system, but rather a 'prophet' who is part of no system. She was someone accountable to 'God' directly, proclaiming things that people do not want to hear, and is in trouble with people a lot of the time. I compared her to the prophet Elijah, who at one point had to rely on ravens to bring him food, so 'on the outs' was he with the established authorities (see 1 Kings 17:1–6). There were those even in my own church who cautioned me against becoming involved with Gloria; their opinions were based on what they read in the paper or heard from other people. Fortunately one of my pastors knew better, and one day when Gloria was in need of a vehicle to transport food from a surplus warehouse in Savannah to THOC, I not only agreed to provide a vehicle, but to drive and to help carry food. It was a lot of food, and a full day's work.

Ironically, during the parts of the week when people need help the most—at night and on weekends—the traditional 'helping' organizations would not have anyone on duty. More than once I observed that the Police would call on Gloria to ask if she could provide temporary lodging for a vagrant individual, which she could and did. It was my job to come get the person from THOC and transport him to a room at a designated local hotel, provided to THOC at a reduced rate.

Observing Gloria's interactions with the people she served was part of my education. She unfailingly greeted and related to people with the love of 'Christ' himself, and was both compassionate and realistic with them. She had an uncanny ability to 'read' people and meet them at their points of need, whether the need was for gentleness or admonition. For my own part I tend to be the 'soft touch' and Gloria would sometimes ask me, "Why do you always stick up for bad people?" Of course she would tell me also that I helped her appreciate the potential for good in some of them.

Sometimes my 'volunteer' work would extend beyond what I had expected to do on a given day. When Gloria would give me an additional task she would sometimes say: "If you do this for me I will never ask you for nothing' else" with an innocent little smile. That always broke me up and I still laugh when I remember it.

I had thought that I would retire in Hinesville and take work as a counselor part-time and as a physician assistant part-time (which is my profession). However the Army had yet another opportunity for me to move, to a wonderful location no less, stay employed by them, and perhaps get a promotion. It was a little difficult to anticipate saying goodbye to good friends and brothers and sisters in the church, but I dreaded telling Gloria I might be moving (at this point I still had some choice in the matter). I had expected her to be disappointed and try to talk me into staying, but when I did call her she asked simply, "That's good ain't it?" putting my concerns to rest and confirming the decision to move.

In the years since we left Hinesville we've kept in touch by phone and through my oldest son who stayed in the community to start his own family and career. I enjoy telling others the story about Gloria and 'The Heart of Christ, Inc.' because I can tell about the opportunity for me to finish my college course, about the opportunity to meet and talk with some of the loveliest people I've ever met. I can relate how it never seemed to work out for her to form relationships with other helping organizations or churches, and how she is like the prophet Elijah who relied on ravens for food.

To me it is evident that Gloria responds to the prompting of the 'Holy Spirit' and that 'God' is working through her in a special ministry. Of course we all have our faults and flaws. The Bible tells us "all have sinned" (Rom. 3:23). Gloria has written hers into a book—how many of us would do that? Not me!

The Bible tells us that "Not many of you [believers in the early Church] were wise by human standards; not many were influential; not many were of noble birth. But 'God' chose the foolish things of the world to shame the wise; 'God' chose the weak things of the world to shame the strong" [1 Cor. 1:26b, 27]. If you think about it, Hollywood loves this theme! Of course they mock 'Christian' people and the church, but they make movie after movie where the unlikeliest people emerge as heroes and save the day. Gloria is such an unlikely—and unrecognized—hero.

I thank 'God' for Gloria and the opportunity to observe, both in the past and the present, how she ministers to persons to whom no one else could minister, and who would not otherwise realize their hope in 'Christ Jesus.' In a world that has plenty of pretenders and 'fallen angels' who invite skepticism and cynicism toward the Church, it is reassuring to all of us when we observe one of 'God's chosen genuinely carrying out His work. As noted above, not everyone sees 'God' at work in Gloria, and that's all right; I see it and it has been one of the great blessings in my life."

-Ronald Ellyson

Made in the USA
Middletown, DE
16 March 2018